The Way The World Is

The Revd John Polkinghorne, ScD, FRS, was until 1979 Professor of Mathematical Physics in the University of Cambridge, a position which he resigned in order to train for the Anglican ministry. Ordained a priest in 1982, he has subsequently served as a curate in Bedminster, Bristol. He is a life Fellow of Trinity College, Cambridge, and has the distinction of being currently the only Fellow of the Royal Society in holy orders. His previous publications include, besides many learned papers and monographs, a semi-popular account of elementary particle physics, *The Particle Play*.

John Polkinghorne

The Way The World Is

The Christian perspective
of a scientist

TRI∆NGLE

First published 1983
Triangle
SPCK
Holy Trinity Church
Marylebone Road
London NW1 4DU

The Scripture quotations in this publication are from
the Revised Standard Version of the Bible, copyrighted
1946 and 1952 by the Division of Christian Education of
the National Council of the Churches of Christ in the USA

British Library Cataloguing in Publication Data

Polkinghorne, John
    The way the world is.
    1. Christian life——Anglican authors
    I. Title
    248.4′83   BV4501.2
    ISBN 0-281-04031-1

Filmset, printed and bound in Great Britain by
Hazell Watson & Viney Ltd, Aylesbury, Bucks

To My Mother
and the Memory of My Father

Contents

Preface

I believe that Christianity affords a coherent insight into the strange way the world is. In this book I try to give an account of this belief and Chapter 1 explains my motivation for the task. Because I have been a scientist the analogies which occur most readily to me are drawn from that discipline. I do not think that this is a far-fetched procedure for, as I try to explain, I believe that science and religion have more in common than is often recognized. However, there is a danger in a book treating both topics, that one will make passing references which will not be clear to every reader. Rather than congest the text with undue weight of explanation, I have relegated some background notes to a glossary. (Words asterisked in the text are included in the glossary.)

Any theologically trained person who reads these pages will readily identify the sources of many of my ideas. I would like particularly to express my indebtedness to the writings of Professor J. Moltmann and Professor W. Pannenberg, and the lectures and writings of Professor C. F. D. Moule. I hope that such a reader might nevertheless derive some modest interest from what I have to say. If so, it would be due to the spectacle of someone with scientific training and experience approaching the issues of religion.

At joint meetings of scientists and theologians which I have attended, it has seemed to me that the scientists have tended to be less sceptical than a section of the theologians. Indeed certain theologians, who appear to see their task as saving Christianity in an age of science, are just those whose ideas make little appeal to me. They seem obsessed with what it might be reasonable to suppose. That has never been a very fruitful method of attack in science, whose principal question has always been, What is it that we have evidence to think is actually the case? The world is complex, full of surprises, and understanding it often involves notions a good deal more subtle than we could possibly have foreseen. Our powers of reasonable prevision are pretty myopic. That is certainly the experience of science, and it would be improbable in the extreme if it did not prove to be the case with religion also. Better a fragmentary grasp of reality than a tidy construction based on a priori oversimplification.

The theologians who appear to me closest in spirit to scientists, in that their ideas arise from the phenomena rather than being imposed upon them, are the New Testament theologians. A good deal of what I have to say is concerned with assessing the evidence about Jesus and his impact upon his first followers. As I indicate from time to time, New Testament scholars have scarcely been unanimous in their conclusions. Like everyone else, in the end I have to follow my own judgement, though I believe that I do not adopt any significant position which would not have the support of some scholars of reputation.

It is a familiar experience in science that in the first-generation exploration of a new regime there emerges a broad idea which casts valuable light on the shape of the phenomena being investigated. (The idea that matter is composed of quarks and gluons is a contemporary example.) The second-generation task, of the detailed exploitation of that idea, is often difficult, tedious and quantitatively only partly successful with the techniques at one's disposal. (Solving quantum chromodynamics will not be easy.) At that stage a certain disillusion and disgruntlement is liable to set in, which unfairly devalues the insight afforded by the original notion.

In the same way there are, I believe, certain general insights into the New Testament evaluation of the 'Christ-event' (to use a convenient, if unattractive, term) which should be held on to and not allowed to disappear under the high magnification and small field of the detailed scholarly microscope. It is these broad insights, as I have been able to discern them, that I have tried to make the basis of my discussion.

Since this book is concerned with an attempt to give a reasoned account of the Christian view of the world, it necessarily tries to indicate the relationship of such a view to other descriptions of the way things are. I have included some material relevant to questions of science and religion, which is mostly contained in Chapters 2 and 3. However, the principal purpose I am here trying to achieve is, so to speak, a scientist's articulation of his understanding of the religious side of that frontier region. It did not seem appropriate to attempt a detailed analysis of the traffic across the border; though I hope I may have an opportunity to attempt that on another occasion.

I wish to thank Dr Michael Rodgers for casting an unbelieving eye over the manuscript and making some useful comments, Mr Robin Brookes for doing the same from a believing standpoint, and Miss Myrtle Powley and the editorial staff of SPCK for their help in preparing the manuscript for publication.

Trinity College
Cambridge
April, 1982

ONE

Apologia

Until 1979 I had spent my entire working life as a theoretical physicist concerned with the study of elementary particles, the basic constituents of matter. It was a very enjoyable life. I did not make any important discovery myself but I had a ringside seat during a period in which many very remarkable and exciting discoveries were being made, leading in due course to the unravelling of a new level in the structure of matter, the level of quarks and gluons.* In the humbler task of the detailed formulation and exploitation of these ideas I was able to make a few useful contributions. I had the very considerable pleasure, with my Cambridge colleagues, of helping pass on this heritage of knowledge to successive generations of very able students and of guiding some of them in their first steps in research. What more could one ask for?

But theoretical elementary particle physics, like most mathematically based subjects, is very much a young man's game. As I approached my fiftieth birthday I was conscious that some change of activity was becoming necessary. As I thought about it, and talked it over with my wife, I reached the really rather surprising conclusion that I should seek to train for the ordained ministry of the Church. I have always stood within the community of the Christian faith, and Christianity has always been central to my life. However it did not necessarily follow from that, of course, that I should turn my collar round. I had regarded the period I had spent as a particle physicist as a Christian vocation, and I still do.

Although I only resigned my Cambridge professorship

from October 1979, the news that I was going to do so was public for at least a year beforehand as I wound up my academic affairs. During that time I had a number of conversations with physicists from all sorts of backgrounds – a subject like particle physics is a sort of international intellectual village in which we all know each other. My friends were naturally rather surprised at my decision and I was mostly trying to explain to them why I had taken it. For a number, the basic question was not why I was seeking ordination but why I was a Christian at all. (There are a significant number of Christian believers in particle physics but, as elsewhere, we are in the minority.)

As I tried to give them some sort of answer I was conscious of a difficulty. It was that, if I were to give any coherent account of my Christian belief, it involved more factors than could be conveniently summarized in a half-hour chat over a cup of coffee in the lounge of some laboratory canteen. For example, the figure of Jesus is central to my faith, but immediately I say that, I am conscious that there are all sorts of questions – How much do we *really* know about him? Wasn't his claim to special status invented by Paul anyway? – to which I need to give consideration and an answer. My friends' eyes would have glazed over if I had treated them to a post-prandial lecture on New Testament critical studies, but any serious attempt by intellectually-minded people to consider Christianity is going to have to get to grips with those sorts of issues at some time.

Accordingly I felt the need of a book which would show my friends that there is a genuine basis of open and scrupulous inquiry which, if it does not *prove* Christianity (for we are in an area of discourse where no one, believer or unbeliever, has access to knockdown final demonstration), can at least show that it is a coherent and rationally motivated view of the way the world is. Given the great volume of religious publishing, it may seem a sign of stupendous blindness or arrogance on my part that I

2

could not find the book that quite served the purpose for which I wanted it.

Part of the reason, I think, is that those of us with a scientific training think in particular ways, which are slightly different in their emphases from those natural to our arts colleagues. Our first reaction is to ask, 'What is the evidence? What makes you think this might be so?' Since I believe that religion, quite as much as science, is concerned with the way things are, I welcome that sort of approach. The crucial question about a religious statement is not, 'Is it comforting? Does it help me face life, or death?' It may do so, but that is only possible if one can first answer yes to the vital inquiry 'Is it true?'

Here we encounter a substantial problem. The facts of science are ones on which we can all agree, once the dust has settled in some new line of investigation. I know, of course, that some philosophers will tell you that science is not concerned with knowledge in that naive realist sense at all. They say that its essence is the establishment of correlations or the ability to manipulate. Quite frankly, I think they are mistaken. Despite wise saws about spectators seeing more of the game, there are some aspects of a game which only players can appreciate. I have never known anyone who worked in fundamental science without being motivated by a desire to comprehend the way things are. Understanding is what we are seeking, and it is the overwhelming impression that that is what is being found.

The success of science clearly arises from the fact that it deals with aspects of reality which are at our disposal to manipulate and interrogate. Hence the power of the experimental method and the remarkable way in which questions get settled. At the end of the nineteenth century there were still a few scientists who thought that atoms were just a convenient figment of the chemists' imaginations, and that they did not represent the existence of a real granularity in nature. Nowadays there can be no doubt that matter is composed of constituents, though the atoms themselves have become large composites and it is the quarks and gluons which are currently assigned the fundamental role.

We are right to be very impressed with the degree of agreed insight achieved in such discoveries. When we look elsewhere, the situation is far less satisfactory. In religion, the heresies debated in the fourth and fifth centuries are debated still, in only slightly modern guise. There is not even agreement on the answer to the most basic theological question of all, the existence of God. It seems that people continue to circle the same old philosophico-theological mulberry bush without being able to pick the fruit.

Faced with such a situation, it is natural to feel at times a temptation to agnosticism, to say, 'Let us hold to the certainties of scientific knowledge, and for the rest, let us recognize that it is mere opinion.' Those of us who have worked in the exact sciences are particularly prone to that temptation. Yet it seems to me that to succumb to it would be gravely diminishing, for it would mean the dissolution of all that makes us truly personal. (I consider this more in Chapter 3.) In actual fact none of us lives his life in that way. Nevertheless I believe that in this area lies the nub of what is felt in our age to be the science–religion question. At heart it is not a logical or a philosophical problem, but a psychological one. It is not what scientists say, but the way that they say it; their bright certainties put other sorts of thought into the shade.

The difficulty that we are considering clearly arises from the different style of knowing which the more personal disciplines demand. You cannot treat people as experimental objects to be manipulated, without destroying thereby their personhood. This fact entails a more subtle and elusive approach to personal knowledge than the sciences require, with a consequent lack of universal agreement. Above all, you cannot subject God to experiment. It is no good standing up and saying, 'If there is a God let him strike me down dead.' He does not play that game.

4

So far we have been talking about facts as if they were incontrovertible items, like the assertion that the galvanometer needle moved to 5·4 on the scale. Of course, facts that are of any interest are caught up in a web of interpretation. In all real knowledge there is a continuous interplay between observation and understanding. Popper* was right to point to the fallacy of induction; a million 'for instances' will not give you a theory without something added to them. Without a theoretical point of view, science becomes mere natural history, history becomes mere annals, theology becomes mere credalism. This sort of consideration must have encouraged Einstein to make his celebrated assertion that the fundamental basis of physical science was not to be empirically discerned, but had to be freely invented. I think he overdid it a bit, failing to do justice to the fact that the 'feel' of the scientific endeavour is discovery, not invention – as Newton acknowledged with the metaphor of his being a child on the beach finding pretty pebbles (not sculpting them!). But Einstein had a point.

We cannot escape from theory-making, and the test of a theory is its economy and coherence in the face of the bewildering variety of phenomena. Part of my reason for being a Christian is that I believe that a Christian understanding offers us such a coherent framework, adequate to the perplexing way the world is. I have had the temerity to attempt to write the book which I could not find in the bookshops. It is my personal *apologia* for the faith I hold.

Two difficulties face me in the attempt. One is the difficulty which prompted the whole enterprise: the fact that there are many lines of thought whose convergence needs to be shown if I am to build up a rational ground for my belief. What I could not outline over that cup of coffee has at least to be indicated in the more spacious confines of a book. Even so, I shall have to paint with a broad brush. I shall try to outline the sort of evidence and argument which underlie the various discussions in which we shall be engaged, so that a reader can get some feel for the basis of it all. An exhaustive discussion of every point would produce an intolerably prolix piece of writing. I have indicated in an appendix various accessible and readable sources from which more detail can be obtained on particular questions. I believe that I have played fair, and that I do not make any assertions which I would not be prepared to defend in the face of more searching inquiry. That is not to claim, of course, that I would be able to convince every such inquirer. As I have already said, we have all left the realm of knockdown argument behind.

This first difficulty – the broad brush difficulty – is one I encountered in the only faintly similar enterprise of this character which I have undertaken, which was the writing of *The Particle Play*, a book attempting to convey to the general educated reader what has been going on in elementary particle physics. At least on that occasion, however, I was treating a subject in which I could reasonably claim to be an expert.

My second difficulty is that in the present instance I have to deal with subjects like New Testament criticism, Christology,* soteriology,* and the like, to which many learned men have devoted their lives, and with which I can only claim the acquaintance of the novice student. I have of course tried to benefit from my reading of the labours of the learned (though in a book of this kind I have avoided a rash of scholarly footnotes to make the point). I have also tried to think straight. At bottom, my only defence must be that these topics are too important to be left solely to the experts.

TWO

The Scientific View of the World

In the beginning was the big bang.* The earliest moment in the history of the world that science can conceive is when the universe was concentrated into a single point. As matter expanded from this initial singularity it cooled and successive regimes decoupled from thermal equilibrium. Thus after about three minutes the temperature had dropped to a thousand million degrees. That was cool enough for deuterium to form. The arrival on the scene of this stable composite of a proton and a neutron helped to fix the global balance of hydrogen and helium in the universe for the rest of its evolution. The ratio of three to one then established (see p. 12) is what we still observe today. After that, nothing of great significance happened for several hundred thousand years. By then the temperature had fallen sufficiently for atoms to be able to form, and this had the consequence of decoupling radiation from thermal equilibrium with the rest of the universe. That same radiation, in a form cooled by further expansion, is observable today as the universal 3°K background radiation* discovered by Penzias and Wilson in 1965, a re-echoing whisper from those far-off times some fifteen thousand million years or so ago.

The universe continued to expand. Gravity took over and condensed matter into galaxies and the stars that compose them. In the nuclear cookery within those stars new heavy elements formed, such as carbon and iron, which had not occurred before. Dying stars, in super-nova explosions, scattered these new elements into the environment. When second generation stars

7

were formed by recondensation, their planets could be made of materials which permitted the next big development in the universe's evolution.

On at least one planet, and perhaps on millions, conditions of temperature, chemical environment, radiation, and the chance congregation of simple atoms, permitted the coming into being of quite elaborate molecules with the power of replicating themselves in that environment. In a remarkable interplay of contingent chance (to get things going) and lawful necessity (to keep them going) there had begun a process by which systems of ever-increasing complexity would evolve. On our planet this eventually led to you and me.

In a nutshell that is the current scientific understanding of how things came to be. Of course there are some imaginative constructions in the story, not every detail of which can claim the certainty of established fact. After all it is largely a tale written by the cosmologists, of whom Landau* said that they are 'often in error but never in doubt'. Nevertheless it seems reasonable to me to suppose that the general tenor of the account is correct. It is an astonishing achievement that men have been able to peer so far into the past and to form so coherent a picture of the processes by which the present diversity of the world has come about. The story that the scientists have to tell is a grand and exciting one. It is a story which has to be reckoned with by anyone who seeks to take account of the way the world is.

So much for the past. What about the future? Our sun is burning up its hydrogen. Eventually, admittedly many millions of years hence, it will begin to exhaust its fuel. Then it will move into the red giant stage of stellar evolution, expanding beyond the confines of the solar system and burning up any surviving life in the process. But we live on a small lump of matter encircling an undistinguished star, one of a hundred thousand million such in our galaxy, which is itself not at all remarkable

8

among the thousand million galaxies of the observable universe. To worry about the fate of such a speck of cosmic dust might, on that view, seem intolerably parochial. Let us instead inquire about the expected fate of the universe itself.

Two alternative scenarios seem possible. Which prevails depends upon how much matter the world contains, and because certain degraded forms are invisible to us we are not sure which prediction we ought to choose. There may be enough matter around for its gravitational pull eventually to reverse the expansion of the universe which we now see. In that case the world will in due course contract to a singularity again; what started as the big bang will end in the big plop. Perhaps following that the universe may bounce back into expansion again as part of an unending cycle of expansions and contractions.

Alternatively, there may not be enough matter for the contraction to happen, in which case the expansion will continue unchecked. Concentrations of matter will separate from each other and within themselves contract into gigantic black holes. These latter, after an inconceivably vast period (estimates run up to $10^{10^{76}}$ years; let the numerate tremble at the thought of such immensity of time), will decay by Hawking black-body radiation* to produce the modern version of the heat death of the universe. One way or another, taking the long term view, the prospects do not seem encouraging.

In addition to scrutinizing past and future, we can look at the present and inquire, What is the quality of the world view presented to us by science? What is its 'feel'? I would characterize it in five ways.

Firstly, the world is intelligible. This is so familiar a fact that we take it for granted. It creates the possibility of science. Again and again in physical science we find that it is the abstract structures of pure mathematics which provide the clue to understanding the world. It is a recognized *technique* in fundamental physics to seek theories which have an elegant and economical (you can

9

say beautiful) mathematical form, in the expectation that they will prove the ones realized in nature. General relativity,* the modern theory of gravitation, was invented by Einstein in just such a way. Now mathematics is the free creation of the human mind, and it is surely a surprising and significant thing that a discipline apparently so unearthed should provide the key with which to turn the lock of the world.

It is this fact of intelligibility which convinces one that science is investigating the way things are. Its insights are certainly open to correction. As access is gained to new regimes, profound modifications can be called for. Thirty years ago, when I was a young research student, no one had dreamed of quarks and gluons. Who can feel confident that thirty years hence they will still be seen as the ultimate constituents of matter? Nevertheless the coherence of the inquiry into the structure of matter, the beautiful way in which the properties of previously 'elementary' objects like protons and neutrons find a natural explanation in terms of their new constituents, makes one feel that it is a tale of a tightening grip on an actual reality.

Indeed, in the microworld of quantum mechanical objects which do not possess vizualizable properties like position and momentum, but merely the potentiality for such quantities; where objects yield on experimental interrogation not a certain location 'here', but only a probability to be 'here' and a probability to be 'there' – in such a protean world it seems that intelligibility remains the sole criterion of reality. Dr Johnson can no longer rely on kicking the stone to make his point. For the reality of elementary particles, his modern counterpart has to appeal not to sensation but to understanding.

The theologian, Eric Mascall, put this well in his book *Christian Theology and Natural Science* when he wrote:

the point is that, though a physicist knows the objective world only through the mediation of sensation, the essential character of the objective world is not sensibility but intelligibility. Its objectivity is not manifested by observers having the same sensory experience of it, but by their being able, through their diverse sensory experiences to acquire a common *understanding* of it.

If it is true, as I think it is, that intelligibility is the ground on which fundamental science ultimately makes its claim to be dealing with the way the world is, then it gives science a strong comradeship with theology, which is engaged in the similar, if more difficult, search for an understanding of God's ways with men.

Secondly, the processes of the world seem to depend for their fruitfulness upon an interplay between chance and necessity. A random event (an aggregation of atoms, a genetic mutation) produces a new possibility which is then given a perpetuating stability by the regularity of the laws of nature. Without contingent chance, new things would not happen. Without lawful necessity to preserve them in an environment whose reliability permits competitive selection, they would vanish away as soon as they were made. The universe is full of the clatter of monkeys playing with typewriters, but once they have hit on the first line of *Hamlet* it seems that they are marvellously constrained to continue to the end of at least some sort of play.

To many, this apparent role of chance is a sign of the emptiness and pointlessness of the world. In his book *Chance and Necessity* Jacques Monod wrote, 'pure chance, absolutely free but blind, [is] at the very root of the stupendous edifice of evolution', and he concluded his book by writing:

> The ancient covenant is in pieces; man at last knows that he is alone in the unfeeling vastness of the universe, out of which he emerged by chance. Neither his destiny nor his duty have been written down.

When I read Monod's book I was greatly excited by the scientific picture it presented of how life came to be. As a particle physicist, I found the biochemical details pretty difficult to follow but, assuming them to be correct, they implied that Schrödinger's equation and Maxwell's equations (the fundamental dynamical equations of quantum theory and electromagnetism respectively, which I could literally write down on the back of an envelope) had this astonishing consequence of the emergence of replicating molecules and eventually life. The economy and profundity of that is breathtaking. For me, the beauty that it revealed in the structure of the world was like a rehabilitation of the argument from design – not as a knockdown argument for the existence of God (there are no such arguments; nor are there for his non-existence) but as an insight into the way the world is. It is clear that the different reactions of Monod and someone like myself to the same set of scientific facts must arise from something outside the strictly scientific world view itself. To that we must turn in later chapters.

The third aspect of the world as viewed by science which impresses me, is our increasing realization that there is a delicate and intricate balance in its structure necessary for the emergence of life. For example, suppose things had been a little different in those crucial first three minutes when the gross nuclear structure of the world got fixed as a quarter helium and three-quarters hydrogen. If things had gone a little faster, all would have been helium; and without hydrogen how could water (vital to life) have been able to form? On the other hand, if things had gone a little slower, hydrogen would have predominated. In that sort of universe, super-novae probably would not explode to scatter the equally vital heavy elements from their interiors into the environment. Scientists are aware of a number of critical considerations of this type which, taken together, produce a fairly tight-knit series of constraints on the way the world must be in order that we are here to observe it. They call the collection of these constraints the *anthropic principle*.

It is not easy to assess the significance of the anthropic principle. Discussing it is rather like the old philosophical debate about whether the existence of the cosmos is itself significant and calls for an explanation (traditionally the Creator), or whether it is just one of those irreducible facts from which you have to start. After all, the intellectual buck has got to stop somewhere. As far as the anthropic principle is concerned, do we just say that it is our luck that the world is such that we are here to think about it? If there has been an infinite cycle of initially expanding and then contracting universes, then the fact that we are around in this particular oscillation might be simply due to the fact that in its details it happens to produce the conditions that make that possible. However, the sort of delicate balance that the anthropic principle exhibits does at the very least give us pause in speculating about possible worlds. We all tend to think that had we been in charge of creation we would have made things differently and better. The closely knit character of a world containing life, which science begins to discern, suggests that it would not be as easy to tinker with things as we might have thought, assuming that some regularity and order are to underlie such a world.

After these rather heady considerations my fourth point will seem crashingly naive. The world is awfully big. We inhabit a planet circling an undistingushed star, itself a mere speck in an undistinguished galaxy among the thousand million galaxies of the observable universe. It would, of course, be a vulgar and foolish error to confuse size with significance. Nevertheless there is something chilling about the vastness of the universe in which we are set.

The thought is far from being original or modern. In the seventeenth century, Pascal wrote, 'The eternal silence of those infinite spaces frightens me.' Scholars think that the remark may be less his own view than that of an imaginary interlocutor with whom they believe he was engaged in the *Pensées*. Be that as it may, the question of the immensity of the world was clearly one which exercised him. More than two thousand years before Pascal the same sort of thought had occurred to a Hebrew psalmist:

When I look at thy heavens, the work of thy fingers,
The moon and the stars which thou hast established;
What is man that thou art mindful of him,
Or the son of man that thou dost care for him?

(Ps. 8.3–4)

Of course, the world that we survey today is much larger in space and time than that conceived of by those earlier writers. However, beyond a certain point it seems to me that nothing much is added in effect by extra powers of ten in the ratio of the size of the cosmos to the size of the earth, or the ratio of the duration of the cosmos to the span of human history. I suppose that the least that one could deduce from all this is that, if there is a purpose in the universe (as I believe there is), it is perhaps not exhausted by what happens in the solar system. We should also note that anthropic principle considerations suggest that the universe has to be as big as it is to give a reasonable chance of life developing.

One of the reasons why one needs a world as big as this for life to emerge within it, is because a smaller system would have run its course too swiftly. Time is needed in which to make men. The long-drawn-out story of our evolution is certainly an odd one, with its prodigality, its blind alleys, its competitive replacement of one species by another. For the Jesuit palaeontologist Teilhard de Chardin, the sweep of the process had a grandeur which evoked in him a response of mystical intensity. For his fellow countryman Jacques Monod, it is on the contrary a tale told by an idiot. I should have thought the testimony more ambiguous in isolation than either would concede.

Certainly, as we shall see, the assertion that at the heart of reality there is One who cares will have to look elsewhere for its persuasive evidence. Mankind would be so much more plausibly the work of a benign Creator if it had come into being a mere six thousand years ago in the limited arena of a garden. No doubt it was the nostalgic longing to retain so manageably proportioned a picture which fuelled the unwise zeal with which some contemporary Christians sought to reject the insights that Darwin had to offer. But perhaps the desire to make God into a domestic craftsman is because he is more easily tamed that way. Pascal and the psalmist are wiser than that. In his book *The Foolishness of God*, John Baker wrote of the argument that balks at the smallness of the earth and the vastness of the world, that 'this small anthropocentric criticism is not an argument. It is nothing more than the complaining voice of mean, utilitarian, gutless, heartless, cerebral, twentieth century, profit margin, Western man.'

The final aspect of the world as viewed by science which strikes me, is its self-contained character. It seems to encompass within itself the explanations of those things which go on of which it takes cognizance. The astonishing chain from big bang to nuclear species, to replicating molecules, to you and me, seems to make the point. When Newton created his theory of the solar system moving under universal gravity, it appeared to him that the perturbations which the planets received from their neighbours would eventually tend to accumulate, in such a way that they would destroy the stability of the system and disperse it. It would become more and more wobbly until it finally flew apart. Accordingly he invoked divine intervention, by which angelically applied corrective forces would keep the solar system in being. A hundred years or so later, Laplace* was able to show that the perturbations would in fact tend to cancel each other out, and the system was inherently stable after all. This enabled him to tell Napoleon, when the latter inquired about the absence of God from Laplace's discussion, that he had 'no need of that hypothesis'.

If that was true of the science of the late eighteenth century, how much more does it seem to be true of the science of today. It seems that the only role left for God is the deistic one of lighting the blue touch-paper to set off the big bang, and then retiring. And if the universe is in fact undergoing an infinitely oscillating series of expansions and contractions, then even that modest task is abolished.

But wait a minute. It is not only God who is in danger of disappearing from the scene. I have spoken of five striking aspects of the scientific world-view. There is also a sixth. I have described a world empty of much that is of the greatest significance in our experience. The world of science contains highly complicated meta-stable systems with the power of reproducing themselves, but it does not have any *people* in it. There is scale and mechanism and structure, but where is the appreciation of the grandeur of that scale, the intricacy of that mechanism, the beauty of that structure?

The distinguished theoretical physicist Vicky Weisskopf wrote a book about 'the natural world as man knows it'. He rightly called his book *Knowledge and Wonder*. The experience of wonder at the structure of the world is an authentic part of the scientist's experience. It is the pay-off for all those weary hours of study and all the frustrations and disappointments inescapable in the prosecution of research. But where does wonder find its lodgement in the world as described by science? It is missing, as are our experiences of goodness, beauty and obligation. Yet these experiences are quite as important and quite as fundamental as anything that can be measured in a laboratory or seen through a telescope. I do not believe that these personal experiences are a sort of transient epiphenomenal ripple on the surface of a mechanically unfolding world. Rather I believe that they are vital to our understanding of the way the world is. It is time to leave the impersonal world of science and to survey the realm of personal human experience.

THREE

The Personal View of the World

Beauty slips through the scientist's net. You could take a performance of Bach's *Mass in B Minor* and Fourier analyse the pattern of sound (that is, subject it to the physicist's standard decomposition into component frequencies) until you were blue in the face; but by those means you would never come to appreciate what it is all about. An exhaustive chemical analysis of the pigments of a Rembrandt self-portrait would miss the point of the picture.

Nor is our experience of art to be dismissed as mere emotion. Could ever a word be worse chosen than that 'mere'? It seems to me that the recognition and enjoyment of beauty is as real and primary an experience for us as any we encounter. I know that an element of cultural learning is involved. Classical music or modern painting may not immediately appeal to us, and the art of other civilizations may be even more elusive. Nevertheless, once our eyes or ears have been opened, we can scarcely doubt that something real has been gained. Instant accessibility is no test of truth; it does not detract from the significance of quantum mechanics* that one must serve an apprenticeship to mathematical physics before one can properly understand it. This impression of the authentic character of beauty is reinforced by the feeling of 'givenness' which artists seem to have about the very works which are so individual a creation by them. For me, that is symbolized by those wonderful half-hewn figures of Michelangelo which seem to be struggling to effect their own release from the block of stone which imprisons them.

Another primary element in the personal world is the sense we have of moral obligation. There are certain things which are right, which we *ought* to do. Again, this has slipped through the scientific net. It is commonly recognized that 'ought', in the sense of obligation, and 'is', in the sense of factuality, are distinct concepts not to be deduced from each other. 'What is the case?' and 'Should this be?' are two incommensurate questions. Science has chosen to confine itself to certain categories of facts alone. It seems to me that it is an important consideration about the wider way the world is, that it contains persons for whom the word 'ought' has a meaning.

But, you may say, have you not now entered on very slippery ground indeed? If anthropology has taught us anything, it is surely the extreme cultural relativity of such notions of obligation. Take any deed which we in the West abhor – say, killing and eating one's grandmother. The chances are that the learned know of some tribe in which just such an action is one of the most binding obligations.

The point is a serious one. In reply, I would want to say two things. In many such cases it seems that the point at issue is not a moral but a factual one. The obligation to kill and eat one's grandmother arises from an understanding of the world in which such an action has consequences which make it seem an act for good. What is at issue between us and that far-off tribe is not the question of whether we are under obligation to do the right, but our different understandings of the world which make us evaluate the right differently. The dilemma is a frequent one. A father acknowledges the obligation to love his delinquent child. Does that mean that he subjects the child to healthily corrective discipline, or is the need rather for a more-or-less indulgent warm acceptance? Both actions could have the same moral aim; either might prove well- or ill-judged in a particular instance. We must not confuse the existence of a moral imperative with the difficult task of finding its true fulfilment in a given circumstance. The obligation to love needs wisdom and discernment if it is to be effectively articulated.

The second thing which I would wish to say, is that I believe that statements like 'love is better than hate' and 'people are not to be manipulated as if they were things' are as certain as any I can make.

At this point my socio-biological* colleague taps me on the shoulder. He has the explanation of these moral convictions of mine. They are genetically programmed into me because altruism is an aid to group survival in the struggle for existence. Let us recognize that remark for what it is. It is no scientifically demonstrated fact, but an ingenious suggestion. Caution is all the more necessary because our friend is using a key which appears to open nearly every lock. There is a line of argument which runs: men (or animals) possess property X; they have survived; therefore property X must be an aid to survival and that is all that need be said about it. If altruism is just an aid to survival, it is surprising that those selfish genes have not been more efficient in creating it. The quintessence of our moral experience is that what we recognize that we ought to do, is so often what in fact we do not do. The picture of human evolution is of the rise of a tribe of killer apes who war on their own kind (itself a disturbing enough thought). It has not been shown that the human story is just a saga of genetic self-perpetuation, and quite frankly it strikes me as preposterous to suppose so.

We have taken account of three remarkable aspects of the world. Scientifically we have found it ordered and intelligible. In our life as persons we have encountered the givenness of beauty and the imperative of moral obligation. Are these things just there, or do they have an origin?

A theistic understanding of the world sees God as the common ground of these aspects of his creation, so that the intelligibility of the universe reflects the way our minds, made in his image, apprehend his world; our experience of beauty is a sharing in his joy in creation;

the moral law is an expression of his will and purpose. Such a view seems to me attractive and sensible. I do not, however, think that it is compelling, in the sense that any reasonable man should be expected without delay or shilly-shallying to adopt it. These considerations are no more than straws in a wind which might prove to be the breath of God.

As we look at the world, there are other aspects which put such a theistic view in grave doubt. An inescapable element in our experience as persons is the widespread existence of suffering. None of us is free from it, and many are subject to a degree of pain or deprivation which seems totally unintelligible. Of course, there are those heroic people who surmount dreadful misfortune with an integrity before which one can only be silent. But for many it seems that the screws are tightened beyond the breaking point, and they are crushed or diminished by what has come upon them. There is not only beauty in the world; there is also terror.

Much of the suffering is due to man's selfishness and greed and evil. No one living in this century of exploitation and war and concentration camps could be ignorant of that. There is a disorder in the affairs of men which seems ineradicable. At the humdrum level of our well-meaning but ineffectual lives we find it so. What reflective person thinking over his life would not at times echo Paul's words: 'I do not the good I want but the evil I do not want I do' (Rom. 7.19)? We have come to recognize that our power to love is limited by the extent to which we have ourselves received love. We cannot give enough as parents because we did not receive enough as children. To say that is not to blame our parents, for they themselves were someone else's children. There is an entail on human lovelessness and consequent suffering in the world.

To say this is but to state half the dilemma. When we have subtracted all the great load of suffering which arises from man's inhumanity to man, there remains much which does not seem remotely to be our responsibility.

To whose charge is to be laid the severely handicapped child who will never have a normal human life? The thirty-year-old dying of cancer with half a life unfulfilled? The elderly person whose life ends in the prolonged indignity of senile dementia? If there is a God, surely these things must be his responsibility. It seems that either he who was thought of as the ground of the moral law is not himself wholly good, or he is opposed by other equal and conflicting powers in the world. Either way, the Christian understanding of God would lie in ruins.

I believe that this problem of theodicy,* of understanding God's ways in the light of the mixture of goodness and terror which we find in the world, constitutes the greatest difficulty that people have in accepting a theistic view of reality. For those of us who stand within the Christian tradition, it remains a deep and disturbing mystery, nagging within us, of which we can never be unaware. I shall want to try to say something about the Christian approach to this problem in a later chapter (ch. 7).

For the moment we must turn our attention to another enigma. We have sketched the scientific view of the world and the personal view of the world. But there is only one world. How do these different descriptions of it relate to each other? After all, they meet in us. We are physical objects, ultimately composed of elementary particles. We are also centres of being who respond to beauty and moral obligation, and possess minds capable of discovering the structure of the laws obeyed by those elementary particles of which we are constituted. The paradigm problem is the hoary one of the relationship between mind and brain. That they are related is obvious. A smart tap on the head with a hammer will quickly establish the point. The brain appears to be a physical system analogous to a computer but with immensely greater capacity and subtlety of connection. Although quantum mechanics introduces a certain 'creakiness' into physics compared with the rigid determinism of classical mechanics, these effects are

21

normally only significant for components which are extremely small, of atomic size or less. The neuronal units of the brain seem to be large on this quantum mechanical scale, so the uncertainty principle would not appear to afford scope for the mind to operate as a sort of tinkering ghost in the cerebral machine, rigging the odds to allow free will to operate. In any case there is something intrinsically implausible about such a notion; it does not have the right 'feel' about it.

It is an unsolved puzzle, therefore, how the brain of neurophysiology is related to that stream of conscious thought which is *the* most basic aspect of our experience of the world. The way people tend to discuss these problems is along these lines: There are, they say, different levels of description of the world, corresponding roughly to the size and complexity of the units treated as basic. Most reductionist of all is physics. Above that are the levels of chemistry, biochemistry, biology, psychology, sociology, and so on. At each level new concepts appear which are not reducible to elements found at lower levels, and this gives to each mode of description its own validity and autonomy. The whole is more than the sum of the parts.

Now all this may prove to be right, but I feel some uneasiness in settling for it just like that. One difficulty is that the divisions between the levels seem liable to dissolve under further investigation. Certainly it is hard to see chemistry as anything but physics writ large, with its characteristic concepts matters of convenience rather than necessity. The current thrust of molecular biology is to carry the same sort of understanding from physics into the biological sphere. The real test of a theory of levels would be that it afforded insight into how the different descriptions related to each other and, therefore, the differing circumstance which made each appropriate.

Lying behind that demand is the hope of an analogy with what in physics is called *complementarity*. It is a well-known fact that in quantum mechanics there are a number of different mutually exclusive ways of describing the same physical system. For example, you can choose to know where all the particles are (in which case you do not know what they are doing) or you can choose to know what they are doing (in which case you do not know where they are). The first choice is called configuration space, the second momentum space. It may sound rather mysterious, but in fact we understand it rather well and perceive why it must be so. The relation between configuration space and momentum space, or between any two mutually exclusive descriptions, is called complementarity.

It is tempting to apply this principle more widely and to suppose, for instance, that descriptions of animals as living systems and as aggregates of elementary particles are in fact complementary. Certainly if you tried to decompose an animal into its physical constituents you would kill it. Caution is necessary, however. Complementarity is another of those ideas which, deceptively easily, can be made to appear the key to turn many locks. The successes of molecular biology show how it is possible to extrapolate from physics into at least the anteroom of life, without contradiction. I must emphasize again that, in quantum mechanics, what gives complementarity its explanatory power (rather than being just a way of labelling how things seem to be) is that we do understand how the different modes of description relate to each other, and why the use of one excludes the others.

Nevertheless there are some intriguing hints from within physics itself which might shed some light on this question of level relationships. The theory of measurement* in quantum mechanics requires the existence of classical (that is, dependably Newtonian) measuring instruments with which to monitor the fluctuating fortunes of the fickle quantum world. Certainly such instruments exist – our laboratories are littered with them. However it may come as a surprise to learn that, after more than fifty years of highly successful exploitation of quantum theory, it is still a matter of dispute how measurement occurs in a consistent way within the formalism.* There are even people who think that a fully consistent scheme will have to take account of the intervention of the consciousness of the observer. I have to say that I think that there are grave difficulties about that particular resolution of the difficulty, but if it were to prove correct it would indicate a remarkable enmeshing of consciousness with the physical world, a significant step away from the absolutely impersonal character of physics. At the very least, I think, one can say that the problem of measurement in quantum mechanics involves a problematic shift of level within physics itself, from uncertain microscopic objects to certain measuring devices.

There are also other aspects of quantum theory (for those in the know, I am referring to the Einstein-Podolsky-Rosen paradox*) which call in question the extent to which fundamental physics can carry out its prime technique of 'divide and rule', that is, split objects up into as small isolated units as possible.

Even classical Newtonian physics contains some surprises. The Belgian theorist, Ilya Prigogine,* who won the Nobel Prize in 1977 for his work on non-equilibrium thermodynamics, has shown that complex dynamical systems exhibit a kind of thermodynamic uncertainty. For example they are characterized by unique direction of time, corresponding to increasing entropy,* in contrast to the simpler systems whose dynamical behaviour corresponds to laws in which time flows freely either backwards or forwards. The possibility of backward flowing time may sound a crazy option – after all, our experience of the past and future is manifestly asymmetric – but it has long been recognized that the *basic* laws of classical mechanics (and almost all the basic laws of quantum mechanics) do not require that unique direction of the 'arrow of time'* which is our common sense way of experiencing the world. All this is very exciting. In the distinction between complex thermodynamic* systems, with a definite direction for their evolution in time, and the time-symmetric basic systems that compose them (as

Prigogine proposes it), we seem to be recognizing *and understanding* the emergence of a level difference of the type that we have been groping for.

It is too early to be sure that ideas of this sort will provide all the clarification we would like of level relationships in the different descriptions of the world. A questing agnosticism may be the best that we can manage about the answers to many of the issues. Unsatisfying as that may be, I do not think that it is disastrous. In trying to understand the way the world is we must hold fast to primary knowledge, whether provided by scientific investigation or through personal experience, even when we do not always understand how two apparently conflicting insights can be reconciled with each other. No progress will be made by a procrustean oversimplification which ignores one insight in favour of the other. It is the sign of a mature discipline that it is able to endure (if not welcome) apparent paradox in the material it considers. A tale from physics illustrates the point.

Isaac Newton believed that light was a stream of small, fast-moving corpuscles. This explained, for example, the sharpness of shadows. However, in 1801 the Cambridge polymath Thomas Young decisively established light's wave-like character by demonstrating the phenomenon of diffraction. Fundamental confirmation came from the researches of Faraday and Maxwell into electromagnetism, from which it was possible to identify light as the vibrations of the electromagnetic field. Nothing could have seemed more certain than the wave character of light. Its recognition and explanation was perhaps the most splendid achievement of nineteenth-century physical science. It must, therefore, have been something of a shock when the turn of the century brought the work of Planck and Einstein which equally indubitably established that light was composed of particles, or 'quanta' as they called them. No one could conceive of how anything could be both a wave and a particle. The two alternatives appeared contradictory. The paradox was complete. No progress would have been made by suppressing or neglecting half the evidence. Both parties, Young and Maxwell, Planck and Einstein, had to be given their due. For almost twenty-five years physicists lived with an unresolved dilemma. Then, in 1928, Paul Dirac* invented quantum field theory* which perfectly manifested the complementary consistency of the wave and particle points of view.

If the study of science teaches one anything, it is that it is unwise to try to lay down beforehand by pure thought what will actually prove to be the case. Reality is often so much more subtle than we imagine.

FOUR

The Religious View of the World

Among the primary experiences which make up our perception of the way the world is, I would argue that there is a religious dimension which must be taken seriously. It involves the sense that there is an Other and Transcendent Power with whom we have to deal. In the long history of man that Power has been called God, and worship has been the proper response to him. Until comparatively recent times some form of theistic view of the world has been almost universal.

'Ah,' you may say. 'As a matter of historical fact what you say is true. But now we are come of age and have sloughed off those childish fantasies which sought comfort by projecting on to an illusory God our desire for a reassuring father figure. We know now that we are alone. Indeed, people like Feuerbach* have made it clear to us that this knowledge is necessary for man in order to realize his true nature and potential.' Such a thought, of man's heroic isolation in a comfortless universe, underlies the words of Jacques Monod which I quoted earlier. I have the greatest respect for people who live clear-eyed in a world without meaning. However, I believe they are mistaken.

My first reason for saying this lies in the remarkably deep-seated character of the hope that is in us – hope against hope, it may seem, in the face of the world of mixed goodness and terror that surrounds us. Peter Berger has drawn attention to this in his remarkable little book, *A Rumour of Angels*. A young child wakes in the night, crying in distress. His mother goes to him to comfort him and assure him that all is well. 'Don't worry,' she says. 'It's all right.' All right? In a world with cancer and famine and labour camps? The woman is engaged in a monstrous deception! Better to say that we'll do what we can to dodge the pain, even if it is liable to get us in the end. Yet we do not, in fact, react like that. We do not feel that the mother is wrong to echo the conviction that came to Julian of Norwich* after her remarkable ecstatic visions, that 'all shall be well, and all manner of things shall be well'. I believe that the almost universal endorsement which the mother's action would receive has its origin in a residual religious conviction that remains within us.

Perhaps this explains something which has always puzzled me. Writers treating the problem of evil quite often seem to find an important clue in the notion that in some way evil is unreal, because it is the absence of the good rather than the presence of a positive quality, just as a shadow is caused by the absence of light rather than the presence of darkness. You find this point of view, for instance, put very strongly by Augustine* in Book VII of the *Confessions*. I have always found it an extraordinarily difficult point to grasp. How could one say to a survivor of Auschwitz, or someone dying of lung cancer, that their experiences were simply an absence of good? But because there is this deep-rooted feeling (everything notwithstanding) of the impermanence of evil and the ultimate and almost unimaginable triumph of good, it may be that these writers are nevertheless on the right track. If so, this hope must surely be rooted in something or someone beyond the immediate flux of experience that we described in the last two chapters.

A second reason for taking the Transcendent seriously begins with my own experience of prayer and worship. However fitful and elusive my experience of God may be, it is not to be denied. That of itself could be of little help or relevance to one of my readers. But there is a great army of people who would say the same thing, and with much greater power. Included among them are many of the most remarkable people who ever lived. What they testify to is not to be dismissed out of hand. Consider Francesco Bernardone, better known to us as St Francis of Assisi. His loving influence has been widely felt, throughout the world and down the centuries, within the Christian community and outside it. Lord Clark, in his book *Civilisation*, devoted the greater part of a chapter to him. It is instructive to compare that account with other scholarly lives of St Francis, written by Christian believers. Kenneth Clark's picture proves unduly sentimental. Francis' life ended in sorrow resulting from trouble he had with his own order of Friars Minor and he was often tearful in his last years. Francis also had his unattractive side; he was rabidly anti-intellectual and forbade the brothers to possess books. For me it is very important to see Francis in his full humanity, its flaws as well as its splendours. Yet, despite those flaws, Francis was a man from whom great power flowed and continues to flow. It is his witness that that power was not his own, but the gift of the God he faithfully served.

A man of his age would see it that way, you say. Let us then turn our attention to the present. Mother Teresa of Calcutta immediately springs to mind. Perhaps more important, though, are people we actually know ourselves. It is easy to go into a church, look around at the congregation and feel that they are a pretty inadequate advertisement for the astonishing claims of God's power at work which the liturgy is proclaiming. That feeling is probably partly true (for we are all flawed and inadequate and God's grace seems often to work very slowly). It is probably also partly untrue (for we tend to project on to others what we, for one reason or another, wish or expect to see. That funny mousy little old lady in the next pew might on closer acquaintance prove to be a person of remarkable endurance and resource.) Be that as it may, I have to say that in my experience most of the people I know who impress me most as being open to reality, deep in perception, firm in love, are also Christian believers. Of course, not all. I gladly acknowledge these qualities in friends who stand outside the faith. But there does seem to be a special quality in people who live close to God. I think of a country clergyman I know. He is a learned man but his parishioners are mostly very simple people with, perhaps, a stronger folk religion than articulate Christianity. By temperament he is somewhat lugubrious and it might seem to a casual observer that here is a rather sad figure. Yet he is a man of deep prayerfulness and you cannot be long in his company without acquiring a profound impression of authentic humanity and closeness to God.

I once told a non-Christian friend of mine about a nun who had been a student at my lectures before she entered the life of a convent. We had renewed contact and she prays for me and I for her. As he thought about this mathematics graduate milking the cows and praying the daily offices, my friend said to me 'What a wasted life!' He could not have been more mistaken. If you make the acquaintance of those who live the life of a professed monk or nun, you will find that they are not people in a bolt-hole in flight from reality, but they include some of the most clear-eyed people you can meet. It is a worth-while experience to spend some time in the quiet of a religious house.

To talk about the insights of analytic psychology might seem indeed to be putting one's head in the lion's mouth with every expectation of decapitation. We all know that Freud took a distinctly dim view of religion, seeing it as a universal neurosis or illusion. Carl Gustave Jung* was much more positive in his stance, though at times you feel that his anthropomorphic approach is something like a take-over bid. It is impossible to doubt the importance of the investigations which have started in this century into the unconscious aspects of the human psyche. As yet, and perhaps for a very long time to come, we are rather in the position of people scrutinizing maps of the world in the early days of cartography. There is truth in the assertion of those great landmasses lying to the west and east and south of us, but their shapes and characters

30

are very imperfectly discerned. A good deal of the psychic map still has *terra incognita* written on it, and where it says 'here be dragons' there may be no more than frisky lizards (or vice versa). Yet it seems clear that we have recaptured an appreciation of the depth of human nature which was known to earlier ages under different forms and then lost to sight as our strongly intellectualized, ego-conscious, civilization developed. In particular, the analysis of dreams reveals the power of symbols at work in our unconscious, symbols which seem to have an impressive degree of autonomy and universality. After a significant dream we can feel that we have had an authentic encounter which may be hard to interpret but which is not to be gainsaid.

All this, of course, does not of itself establish the truth of a religious view of the world, but by making us aware of more things than we had hitherto taken into account, it encourages a certain openness to the nature of reality.

Of more direct relevance is the claim to mystical experience.* It seems that there are people to be found at all times and in all cultures who have had an overwhelming experience of union with the ground of being. Reading their accounts one is struck by their similarity, despite the divergent circumstances and understandings otherwise found in those who testify. In *The Varieties of Religious Experience* the psychologist William James concluded his survey of the phenomenon by saying:

This overcoming of all the usual barriers between the individual and the Absolute is the great mystic achievement. In mystic states we become one with the Absolute and we become aware of our oneness. This is the everlasting and triumphant mystical tradition, hardly altered by differences of clime or creed. In Hinduism, in Neoplatonism, in Sufism, in Christian mysticism, in Whitmanism, we find the same recurring note, so there is about mystical utterances an eternal unanimity which ought to make a critic stop and think, and which brings it about that the mystical classics have, as has been said, neither birthday nor native land. Perpetually telling the unity of man with God, their speech antedates language, and they do not grow old.

I have never had a mystical experience myself, but I think that the weight of the testimony of those who have is something to which one has to give attention.

FIVE

The New Testament Evidence

The kinds of consideration outlined in the preceding chapters would, I think, incline me to take a theistic view of the world. By themselves that is about as far as they would get me. The reason why I take my stand within the Christian community lies in certain events which took place in Palestine nearly two thousand years ago.

That in itself is a very odd thing to say. Is the true key to the way the world is to be found in the possession of a wandering carpenter in a peripheral province of the Roman Empire, far away and long ago? The experience of science should make one open to the unexpected, aware that apparently slight circumstances may be fraught with large significance. The odd behaviour of a culture near an open window leads to the discovery of penicillin; a tiny separation of two spectral lines in hydrogen (the Lamb shift*) is the trigger to the unravelling of quantum electrodynamics,* the one splendidly quantitatively successful example of a relativistic quantum field theory, matching calculation and experiment to the limits of both of a few parts per million. The claim that in Jesus and the events associated with him, the nature of God and the destiny of men are revealed is a strange one, but it is not to be set aside without careful inquiry.

There are two obvious problems to be faced at the outset of such an inquiry. How good is the evidence on which to base our knowledge of Jesus? And how accessible to us can his world be across the cultural gap of the intervening centuries, how relevant his thought to ours today? We must consider these problems in turn.

The reliable witness that we have about Jesus and his

impact on the world, the details of his life and the contemporary assessments made of him, are all contained in the collection of writings which we now call the New Testament. Naturally, none of the original manuscripts survive, so that a preliminary point to be dealt with is, How well has the text been preserved? The evidence is extremely good. My edition of the Greek New Testament lists among its sources for the Gospels eleven partial papyri manuscripts from the sands of Egypt and dating from the second century onwards, and thirty complete, and a number of partial, uncial manuscripts (that is, early manuscripts written in capital letters), dating from the fourth century onwards. In addition there are very many less important manuscripts; early translations into Latin, Syriac and Coptic; and many quotations in Church writers from the second century onwards. A comparable weight of evidence exists for the other parts of the New Testament. Compare this with the manuscripts available for many classical writers, which are often no better than two or three, dating from many hundreds of years after the original. The New Testament is incomparably the best attested of any ancient writing.

All this great mass of evidence has been patiently sifted through by scholars to establish the best text. There are, of course, many variations in detail between one manuscript and another, due to copying errors and the occasional desire of a scribe to 'improve' the text, usually by substituting a simpler guess for a difficult reading. For example, a great many manuscripts of John 1.18 contain the phrase 'the only-begotten son' but there is good evidence from early manuscripts that this originally read much more mysteriously 'the only-begotten God', whilst in the manuscript called Sinaiticus, which is in the British Library, we can see that a corrector has changed the latter into the easier 'the only God'.

By these sorts of comparisons it is possible for scholars to work out in most cases what the original readings were. You can get a feel for the results of their labours by taking a modern version of the Bible which contains marginal readings, that is, one which lists alternatives at points where the text is to some degree uncertain. Compared with the Authorized Version, which was based on the poor manuscript evidence available in the seventeenth century, there are two or three major deletions. For example, it is now widely recognized that the closing verses of Mark (16.9-20) are a second century addition, quite probably replacing an original ending which has just got lost. However, in the great body of the text, I think you will agree that the uncertainties are very small, and we can feel confident that we have a text which correctly conveys its authors' intentions.

A much more crucial question is the extent to which it truly records the words and deeds of Jesus and the impact that he made on his very earliest followers. Jesus himself, of course, wrote no book, and some years elapsed before the earliest of our documents were written. The crucifixion was probably about AD 30, the earliest New Testament writing is probably Paul's first letter to the Thessalonians written around AD 50, the earliest Gospel Mark, written in the middle sixties.

A word is necessary about the problems of dating. No book of the New Testament carries attached to it its date of origin, so such questions have to be answered by indirect inference. For example, in Mark 13 the author is clearly concerned with an imminent crisis which fits in with the atmosphere leading up to the Roman-Jewish war of AD 66-70, but there is no sign that he knows of the traumatic events of the siege and destruction of Jerusalem by Titus, which was the bloody climax of that conflict. Hence a date in the middle sixties seems indicated, which fits in with an early tradition that this Gospel was written following the death of Peter, earlier in the decade. On the other hand, the related passage to Mark 13 which appears in Luke is felt by many scholars to contain recognizable reference to the details of the fall of Jerusalem (21.20, see also 19.43-44), so that that Gospel is usually dated later in consequence.

The dating of Paul's epistles is attempted by trying to

fit the circumstances they describe into the pattern of his life as we know it. This is complicated by difficulties of detail in squaring Paul's own accounts which he occasionally gives us in his letters (for example Gal. 1.12–2.14) with the systematic life story contained in Acts. The discrepancies are not more than one might expect in writings based on recollections rather than a carefully constructed biographical archive, but they certainly complicate the issue.

In this type of inference, and in many others, New Testament scholarship is closely akin to observational science (as opposed to experimental science). We cannot return to first-century Palestine to interrogate the authors or chief actors, any more than an astronomer can take flight to investigate a quasar* at first hand. In both disciplines an understanding has to be reached on the available evidence interpreted in ways that are sensible and consistent.

Both subjects have been characterized by occasional rash extravagances. Confronted with a new and puzzling phenomenon, some astronomers have been prone to invoke radical changes in the laws of nature, only to find that the problem yielded to patient and persistent work along more conventional lines. (Some of the recent ballyhoo about the admittedly strange dynamical structures revealed in Saturn's rings is an example of this sort of thing happening.) Similarly, New Testament scholarship has had its wilder shores. Both disciplines sometimes find a healthy corrective in new evidence. The great Tübingen scholar F. C. Baur constructed a theory from which he concluded that John's Gospel was written late in the second half of the second century. However, a small papyrus fragment came to light from the sands of Egypt, unmistakably part of a copy of the Gospel, and dated by experts as not later than AD 150 and perhaps significantly earlier. In astronomy and New Testament scholarship alike, it is usually possible eventually to sift out and discard the more bizarre theories.

It is time to return to the question of the reliability of

the New Testament accounts. Let us take the Gospels first. The first three Gospels, Matthew, Mark and Luke, strike even the casual reader as being similar to each other. They are commonly called the synoptic Gospels* because of this common view that they appear to take. The fourth Gospel, John, is manifestly different and we will return to it later.

The similarity of the synoptics is largely due to a great deal of common material. About 90 per cent of Mark appears in closely parallel form in Matthew and over 50 per cent in Luke. Sometimes the verbal agreement is virtually perfect. Take a Bible and compare, for example, Matt. 16.24-25 with Mark 8.34-35 and Luke 9.23-24. Moreover, the order in which the common stories and sayings appear in the three Gospels is pretty nearly the same, though the way in which the extra material is inserted into Matthew and Luke is different. Luke tends to have longish chunks of Mark followed by chunks of his own material, while in Matthew things are more interlaced. When we compare the extra material that is contained in Matthew and in Luke we find again that there is a good deal of common ground between the two. This shared material amounts to over 200 verses and is mostly in the form of sayings of Jesus. Once more we find that the similarity is sometimes almost exact (for example, compare Matt. 3.7-10 with Luke 3.7-9) but at other times this is less the case, varying down to just a common idea with little verbal identity (Matt. 22.1-14 and Luke 14.15-24). There is some agreement of ordering of this material between the two Gospels but it is less striking than for the Marcan material.

The extent of the agreement of detailed wording, and of order where this exists, suggests that these coincidences must have had their origin in the fixed form of written literary sources rather than arising simply from the evangelists drawing on a common fund of recollections of what Jesus said and did. The solution of what those written sources were (that is, the solution of what is called the 'synoptic problem') which has commended itself to most people, is that Matthew[1] and Luke had Mark's Gospel before them (this fits with dating arrived at from other considerations and it seems more likely that they added to him rather than that he condensed one of them, leaving out so much interesting material in the process) and that Matthew and Luke had an additional common source, called by scholars Q,* which was principally a collection of sayings of Jesus. Of course Q is a hypothetical object, like the dark companion of Sirius.* No one has even seen a copy of Q, but it seems a sensible guess that it existed. In addition, Matthew and Luke must each have had some special sources of their own, for each of their Gospels contains significant material which is found nowhere else. For example, Matthew is the only Gospel to tell the parable of the sheep and goats (Matt. 25.31–46) and without Luke we would not have known the parable of the good Samaritan (Luke 10.30–37).

The situation, therefore, is that in terms of written sources we see Mark as a primary source, composed in the middle sixties, and Q another written source, perhaps constructed at much the same time or conceivably earlier (it is clearly hard to date). This leaves a gap of thirty-five years or so between the events and their records, equivalent to looking back on post-war Britain from the present day – not an impossible task, particularly when strange events and a charismatic figure are involved. No doubt you could still collect a good deal of reliable information about Sir Winston Churchill by talking to those who had a chain of contact going back to him. Doubtless in your inquiry you might in addition to genuine reminiscence come across the odd apocryphal story which correctly gave the feel of the man without being strictly historical, and also, perhaps, the occasional story which was just made up.

An important insight into what was happening during

1. We do not know for sure who the authors of the Gospels were. It is quite likely that Mark, the companion of Peter, wrote the second Gospel; extremely unlikely that the apostle Matthew wrote the first. I use the conventional names to denote the unknown authors.

the thirty-five-year gap between the events and the written record is given to us by the curiously named discipline of 'form criticism'.* An examination of the synoptic Gospels shows that they are mostly made up of discrete stories and statements (called by the learned 'pericopes') which are stuck together with some sort of formal connecting link, like Mark's favourite 'and immediately . . .'. A Gospel is built out of pericopeic building blocks. Once you have had this pointed out to you, the fragmentary character of the synoptics becomes very clear, and it contrasts strikingly with the continuity of the passion narratives at the end, which we shall have to consider in Chapter 7. The form critics study these basic blocks and classify them into different types: pronouncement stories leading up to a punch line delivered by Jesus (such as Mark. 3.31–35 which reaches a climax in the saying 'Whoever does the will of God is my brother and sister and mother'); miracle stories which usually end with the astonished reaction of the bystanders (Mark 1. 23–27, etc.); collections of sayings with common themes (Matt. 6.5–18, prayer and fasting) or common catchwords for easy remembering (Luke 16.9–13, 'mammon'); and so on. It seems natural to assume that these units circulated separately in the oral tradition for a long while before being collected together into written compilations, and so they take us well into that thirty-five-year gap. The question is, how far?

One thing which form critics also study is what, in their Germanic way, they call the *Sitz im Leben*, the 'situation in life' of a particular pericope. What they mean by that is: Why were these particular stories or sayings remembered? I would incline to the view that it was quite often simply because they were intrinsically memorable. Jesus was the sort of man who produced indelible impressions on people, the power of which survived the telling to others. Just recall those Gospel sayings or stories which you yourself remember – the parable of the good Samaritan; the healing of the paralysed man let down through the roof by his four friends; the words 'I say to you that every one who looks on a woman lustfully has already committed adultery with her in his heart'; the marvellously discerning reply to those who asked about paying tribute money to the Romans, 'Render unto Caesar the things that are Caesar's and unto God the things that are God's' – they do have a self-perpetuating vividness, do they not? Nevertheless, the form critics doubtless have a point in suggesting that sometimes, perhaps often, it was because a pericope spoke to some particular need or perplexity in the life of the early Christian community that it came to be treasured and repeated. That is what is meant by its situation in life, its point of application to the life of those first Christians.

This realization immediately raises a critical question about the value of the New Testament evidence for the words and deeds of Jesus himself. Have they been so filtered, and thereby distorted, by the attitudes of primitive Christianity, that their true original form and balance is lost? The hoary *canard* that Paul is the founder of Christianity is an extreme example of this type of thinking. To put it bluntly, if less extravagantly, are many of Jesus' sayings just the creation of the early Church?

There seems little doubt that a process of this sort, involving the intervention of the primitive community, took place to some degree. (I will have more to say about how to evaluate it in Chapter 9.) In the story of the rich young ruler in Mark 10.17–22, Jesus' reply to the young man's question 'Good teacher, what must I do to inherit eternal life?' is given as 'Why do you call me good? No one is good but God alone'. This is a difficult saying. Is Jesus repudiating the reputation of goodness which is so much part of the Gospel testimony to his character? I personally believe that he is replying to the young man's effusiveness by pointing to God as the sole source of all true goodness; it is characteristic of the earthly Jesus that his concern is to do the will of his heavenly Father. Be that as it may; when Matthew came to incorporate this incident into his Gospel (Matt. 19.16–22) he obviously felt the difficulty, for he toned down the first part of

Jesus' reply into the innocuous 'Why do you ask me about what is good?', a sort of donnish philosophical-chat answer which is quite uncharacteristic of Jesus. Clearly some changes *were* made in the words of Jesus by New Testament writers.

Equally, I believe, we can see that sometimes words were attributed to him which he is extremely unlikely to have spoken. In Matt. 18.15-18 Jesus is represented as giving detailed instructions about how a Christian congregation should deal with a member who falls into flagrant sin. He is to be rebuked first privately, then in the presence of two or three witnesses, finally in the presence of the whole church, after which, if he is still unrepentant, he is to be cast out. Jesus preached the coming of the Kingdom of God* (ch. 6) and it is very improbable that he gave precise instructions for future ecclesiastical discipline. It is natural to suppose that these words were created by someone in Matthew's community, doubtless after much prayer and meditation, as representing what it was believed Jesus would have said in the face of the particular problem of church order which perplexed that congregation.

Thus we have reason to believe that the early Christian community has left its impress on the accounts of Jesus which we find in the synoptic Gospels. The vital question is, to what degree? Has that impression largely defaced the original image?

In the first flush of the form critical movement the Oxford scholar R. H. Lightfoot wrote:

> It seems, then, that the form of the earthly no less than the heavenly Christ is for the most part hidden from us. For all the inestimable value of the Gospels, they yield little more than a whisper of his voice; we trace in them but the outskirts of his ways.

Quite frankly, I think that's absurd. Anyone who has worked in an academic discipline knows that scholars can so get the bit between their teeth that they pursue a point of view with a monocular relentlessness which soon takes them beyond the bounds of common sense. Read one of the Gospels or, better still, read all three synoptics. Do you feel that they convey the strong impression of a remarkable personality, or are they the creation of early Christian committees? For me there is no doubt about the answer. There is something remarkably implausible in the notion that Jesus was the sort of person who leaves little recognizable trace and that most of the striking conceptions and insights which the Gospels contain are the product of the life of the primitive community.

This belief, that there is a firmly reliable original stratum within the gospel tradition, finds confirmation from a number of considerations.

First-century Palestine was a society in which oral transmission had an accuracy and importance which it is hard for us to realize today. The Rabbis' teaching was handed on in this manner. When the teaching of Jesus is translated out of the Greek of the Gospels into the original Aramaic* which he would have spoken, it is often found to take a rhythmically poetic form conducive to easy memorization – the idea of the advertising jingle put to better use. There is, therefore, nothing improbable in the accurate preservation of many of his sayings.

Moreover, there is clear evidence of the authority and respect accorded to the words of Jesus, even when they were difficult or uncongenial. We have already noted Mark's transmission of the odd remark 'Why do you call me good?' and both he and Matthew report the strange and terrible cry from the cross, 'My God, my God, why hast thou forsaken me?', words so mysterious and chilling that it was found necessary to quote them also in their original Aramaic as a preservation of the true voice (Matt. 27.46, Mark 15.34).

Equally we can detect in the evangelists a respect for telling a story the way it happened. All four Gospels preserve a detailed circumstantial account of Peter's threefold denial of Jesus. Only a strong regard for truth could account for so insistent a presentation of this highly embarrassing story about a figure of great importance in the early Church.

Although the Church may sometimes have created words of Jesus to meet its present preoccupations, it certainly did not do so without limit. Acts and the Epistle to the Galatians make it clear that a major problem in the early Christian community was the question of whether Gentile believers had to submit to the Jewish rite of circumcision. How easy, one would think, to invent a word of the Lord to settle the issue and so confirm the solution otherwise arrived at. There is no such word in the Gospels.

There are times when it is hard to decide whether a word of Jesus is original or a subsequent creation. A notorious example is the extra saying to Peter at Caesarea Philippi found only in Matthew (16.18), 'You are Peter and on this rock I will build my church'. The Lord's confirmation of the natural leader of his disciples, or a *post facto* authentication of the Petrine party in the early Church? I can't make up my mind about that one. There are bound to be some grey areas, but I believe that we can find in the Gospels the basis for a reliable account of Jesus' words and deeds. The next chapter will have more to say about the nature of the picture so obtained.

It is time to recall that the earliest writings of the New Testament are not the Gospels but some of the epistles of Paul which were written during that gap period we have been discussing. Moreover, they contain within themselves much older material which the apostle says he is quoting. In the first epistle to the Corinthians, written about AD 55, Paul reminds his readers that when he founded their church he

> delivered to you as of first importance what I also received, that Christ died for our sins in accordance with the scriptures, that he was buried, that he was raised on the third day in accordance with the scriptures, and that he appeared to Cephas [that is, Peter],

then to the twelve. Then he appeared to more than five hundred brethren at one time, most of whom are still alive, though some have fallen asleep. Then he appeared to James, then to all the apostles. Last of all, as to one untimely born, he appeared also to me.

(1 Cor. 15.3–8)

When Paul speaks of having 'received' this early Christian statement, it is natural to suppose that he is referring to instruction he received after his dramatic conversion on the Damascus road. This is likely to have occurred three or four years after the crucifixion, so that the material reported in those opening verses of 1 Cor. 15 is very early indeed.

In the eleventh chapter of the same epistle Paul refers to an account of the Last Supper which he says he received 'from the Lord' (1 Cor. 11.23–26), presumably meaning that his knowledge extended to the witness of those who could claim to testify to the words of Jesus on that occasion. There is also other material present in the epistles which is not cited as quotation but which, from style and form, scholars believe is probably pre-Pauline. This includes the remarkable hymn of Christ's self-humiliation from heavenly glory to obedient death on a cross, followed by his exaltation to Lordship, found in Phil. 2.6–11, and, perhaps, the well-known description of love (*agapē*) in 1 Cor. 13.

As far as one can trace it back – and some of this material goes very far back indeed – one finds most remarkable assertions being made about Jesus by his followers. We shall have to consider the significance of this in more detail in the following chapter.

You may wonder why, in this discussion of the earliest followers of Jesus, I have not referred to the testimony of Acts, which appears to give an account of the Church from its emergence at Pentecost onwards. Acts is one of the books of the New Testament about which there is the greatest scholarly controversy, as to its date of composition and the historical reliability of its material. Is its author (as the preface to his Gospel, Luke, claims) one who writes an 'orderly account' based on the evidence of those 'who from the beginning were eyewitnesses and ministers of the word' (Luke 1.1–4) – in a word, is he the first real Church historian? – or is he writing late in the first century and imposing on his material a picture derived from the different circumstances of his own day? Some say one, some say the other. Personally, I believe that Luke is historically trustworthy. Research has shown how accurate is his knowledge of relevant local style and custom as recorded in his account of Paul's missionary journeys. Of course, he writes up his material in a free style, composing speeches to summarize what Peter or Paul said on various occasions, in a manner which will be familiar enough to readers of the contemporary Jewish historian, Josephus; but I believe there is much underlying early and valuable tradition preserved by Luke. However, because the point is controversial, it seems best to rely on Acts as little as possible for our present purpose.

Finally, we must turn our attention to 'the fourth Gospel'.* The coyness of the phrase commonly used by scholars to refer to the Gospel of John is itself an indication of its peculiar character. We do not normally feel the need to refer to Mark as 'the second Gospel'.

The Gospel of John is for me the most remarkable book in the New Testament. Partly that feeling derives from its profoundly ironic awareness of the significance which underlies the surface appearance of events. Jesus says, 'I, when I am lifted up from the earth, will draw all men to myself', a grim pun on exaltation and crucifixion (John 12.32). Caiaphas, plotting the death of Jesus, unwittingly utters a prophecy when he says, 'It is expedient for you that one man should die for the people' (John 11.50). Partly it is the dialectic skill with which conversation is handled. Read in John 4 Jesus' conversation with the Samaritan woman, with its shifting levels of meaning and the courteous probing of the woman's real thoughts and circumstance. But above all, there is the figure of Christ himself, the words he utters, pregnant with power and a strange hope: 'I am the way, the truth and the life' (John 14.6); 'I am the resurrection and the life' (11.25); 'I am the light of the world (8.12), the good shepherd (10.14), the true vine (15.1)'. It is like the timeless utterance of a Byzantine icon of the Pantocrator.

The Johannine Christ is a profoundly impressive figure. The trouble is that the impression is so different from that which we receive of the Jesus portrayed by the synoptics. One speaks with the accents of eternity. The other, with his pithy sayings and vivid parables, seems firmly rooted in the soil of Palestine. There is little difficulty in deciding which picture is the more historically persuasive. That impression is confirmed when we notice that in the fourth Gospel everyone talks in these timeless tones – John the Baptist, and even Jesus' opponents, as well as the Lord himself.

This different quality of John's Gospel was apparent from early times. At the end of the second century Clement of Alexandria wrote:

> Last of all John, perceiving that the external facts had been made plain in the gospel [that is, the synoptics] composed a spiritual gospel.

However, the situation is more subtle than the simple equations, synoptists = history, John = spiritual significance, would suggest. For one thing, scholars have come to realize that there are theological concerns at work in the way the synoptic Gospels are put together. Some of the patterns they have sought to uncover have no doubt been unduly imaginative, like the over-interpretation of Shakespeare by the more fanciful critics. But the Gospels of Matthew, Mark and Luke are certainly not artless aggregations of pericopes. The theological purpose of a sequence like Mark 8.22–30, in which a miracle story of the opening of a blind man's eyes is followed by Peter's realization and confession at Caesarea Philippi that Jesus is the Christ, is clear to see.

Equally, detailed study reveals a strong concern in the fourth Gospel with a source of historical tradition largely independent of that found in the Mark–Q nexus of the synoptics. John does, after all, claim to incorporate eyewitness evidence (John 19.35, 21.24). As an example of John's historical interest, consider the aftermath of the feeding of the five thousand, the only miracle* recorded in all four Gospels. Whatever happened on that mysterious occasion, it is clear in the synoptics (Matt. 14.22, Mark 6.45) that when it was over Jesus packed off the disciples with indecent haste before turning to the disposal of the crowd. His behaviour seems strange, and without the clue provided by John it would be unintelligible. The fourth evangelist tells us that the crowd were so impressed by what had happened that their always smouldering hopes of a political messiah were kindled and they were tempted to 'take him by force to make him a king' (John 6.15). In this highly explosive situation we can understand that Jesus' first concern was to protect the integrity of his immediate circle, lest they too should fall under the freedom-fighter spell. Another instance of John's concern for a factual basis for what he writes is provided by the observation that his Gospel has many more named locations for events, compared with the rather vague topography of the synoptics. The detail in this respect is good; excavations have confirmed the existence in Jerusalem of a pool with five porticoes, just as described in John 5.2.

It appears, therefore, that the question of historicity in the fourth Gospel is more complex than might have appeared at first sight. Nevertheless, I do not doubt that the way Jesus appeared to his contemporaries is much more faithfully mirrored by the figure portrayed by the synoptists than by the majestic presence of the Johannine Christ. If this is so, it disposes of an attempted knockdown argument which you sometimes hear quoted to prove the divinity of Jesus. The argument runs that he claimed to be God and so he must either have been deluded ('mad') or deceiving ('bad') or right ('what he said he was'). Since the first two are unthinkable the third must be correct. Even a man with so acute a mind as C. S. Lewis seems to have been brought to Christian belief along this route. (Any working scientist knows that bad arguments can lead to correct conclusions!) The difficulty lies in establishing the premise, that Jesus said he was God. Even the evidence of the fourth Gospel is puzzling on this point. Though he is represented as claiming a unique unity with God ('I and my Father are one' (John 10.30)) and as taking on his lips the Old Testament name of the living God when he said 'Before Abraham was *I am*' (John 8.58, cf. Exod. 3.14) – actions which led the Jews to take up stones to execute the punishment for blasphemy – yet he is also found saying, 'For my Father is greater than I' (John 14.28); and God is repeatedly referred to by him as 'the one who *sent* me', implying a subordinate role. But even were the evidence less enigmatic it would be unsafe to ground the argument on the historically uncertain utterances of the Johannine Christ. In the synoptics we do not find such categorically explicit claims, though I shall want to draw attention in the next chapter to the significance of the remarkable implicit authority with which Jesus claims to speak.

Now for the second problem posed by our New Testament inquiry: Is not the thought world of the New Testament so different from ours today that the former can really have little to say to us? Has not first-century Palestine sunk below our intellectual horizon?

No one can deny that there are great differences between the two worlds and that we have reason to believe that, at least in some respects, our own understanding is vastly superior to theirs. Our picture of the physical world is unquestionably an improvement on the three-decker universe they inhabited. Nor, of course, do we attribute epilepsy to demon possession.

Certain ways of argument in the ancient world are totally without force for us. The unknown author of the epistle to the Hebrews bases an argument (9.15–17) on the fact that the same Greek word (*diathēkē*) means both covenant (that is, God's promise) and also a will. However persuasive that might have been to the rabbinic mind, it cuts no ice with us. Once again, however, the suspect quality of an argument does not necessarily imply the falsity of its conclusion – in this case, that the death of Jesus is the source of liberty for men. After all, Copernicus put the sun at the centre of the solar system because to do so gave a scheme more elegant in circular terms than Ptolemy's, and Copernicus was certain that heavenly bodies must be in circular motion.

Two considerations prevent us from writing off first-century Palestine as a modern irrelevancy. The first is the proven power of great minds and personalities to speak across yawning cultural gaps. We are quite far removed even from the England of Elizabeth I, and ancient Athens is as remote from us culturally as first-century Jerusalem. Yet who can doubt that Shakespeare, and Plato and Aristotle, and the Greek tragedians, still have power to illuminate our minds and stir our spirits? In the same way, I believe that the open-minded reader of the New Testament will find he is addressed in many ways that speak powerfully to him.

The second consideration is one emphasized by Peter Berger in a chapter of *A Rumour of Angels* called 'Relativising the Relativisers'. We have come to see how the cultural framework of a particular civilization provides a matrix for people's perception of the world, so that the way the world seems is partly determined by culture: where I see a snake an Australian aborigine beholds the spirit of his grandfather. No doubt this realization puts a question mark over one's account of the world, though I think that common sense indicates that it is in the nature of a caution rather than a statement of impossibility. We see the cultural relativity of other civilizations rather clearly. What we do not always see quite so clearly is that it is not only *their* perceptions of the world that are in question, but also *ours*. It may well be that we have lost some vital clues to an understanding of the way the world is. Some study of the thought of other ages is necessary to free us from the relativistic prison of our own age.

We live in a privatized, individualistic world. The concept of human solidarity, so familiar in ancient Israel or tribal Africa, is almost lost to us. Whatever John Donne may have said, the pressure of the present age is to live as an island, an island not even recognized as joined beneath the ocean of the subconscious to the other islands of the human archipelago. This notion of some degree of human solidarity is one which we need to recover; as I shall argue in Chapter 7.

Perhaps this sort of consideration also helps us with a problem which many modern readers of the New Testament find peculiarly acute. It arises from the strangely spirit-filled world which we encounter in its pages. I do not mean just the attribution of certain forms of disease to demon possession, for I think that here we meet with something which, without denying the psychosomatic element in illness, is rather easily set aside where necessary. Rather I mean the notion, so important to Pauline thought, that there are non-human authorities and powers at work in the world (1 Cor. 15.24); that 'we are not contending against flesh and blood but against the principalities, against the powers, against the world rulers of the present darkness, against the spiritual hosts of wickedness in the heavenly places' (Eph. 6.12), even though they cannot separate us from 'the love of God in Christ Jesus our Lord' (Rom. 8.38–39) because Christ possesses an over-ruling authority (Col. 1.15–17), which was manifested when 'he disarmed the principalities and powers and made a public example of them, triumphing over them' in his cross (Col. 2.15).

All this is powerfully emotive language but utterly strange to a twentieth-century reader, who may well feel very put off by it. Is it just a fanciful way of using mythology* to say that there is good and evil about us and that the example of someone like Jesus is a help in our attempts to do the right thing? Or is it conceivably, as Paul and his friends certainly thought, some actual expression, doubtless imperfectly articulated, of the way the world is? Jungian studies of depth psychology seem to indicate that there are powerful symbols active in the unconscious and manifest in dreams, some light, some dark, some ambivalent, whose continuing recurrence in widely differing circumstances suggests that they possess a degree of autonomy independent of individual men. Jung called them archetypes,* and they are the basis for his postulation of the collective unconscious, the sub-oceanic linkage of the ego islands of men.

An example of such an archetype is the Mother figure. In the worship of the earth goddess, or in certain aspects of the cult of the Virgin Mary, she is presented as a focus for those essential feminine qualities which are in danger of neglect in religions whose symbols are predominantly masculine. A truer insight is to look for these qualities within the one godhead, an insight articulated with startling force by the fourteenth century visionary, Julian of Norwich who, despite a humble desire to be an orthodox daughter of the Church, was bold enough to speak of the Second Person of the Trinity as Jesus our Mother. Detached from their true ground in God such symbols can take on a life of their own, with consequences which may be baleful. The dark side of the Mother is the Witch. Jungians believe that when due allowance has been made for the individual and sociological forces un-doubtedly at work in the seventeenth century witch crazes, there is a residue which can only be attributed to the activity of this dark archetype in the collective unconscious.

It is obviously very difficult to evaluate these archetypal claims, particularly when they involve a symbol like the Mother which is deeply rooted in individual experiences of early childhood. Nevertheless the contemplation of the sad follies and evil deeds committed in the name of cause or country or (one must add) church does seem to indicate the powerful collective force of symbol in the life of men. It does not seem impossible that Paul's disturbingly 'mythical' language is pointing to an element of reality which we need to recover.

SIX

Jesus

Jesus exercises an abiding fascination upon men. There have been innumerable attempts to delineate a portrait of him. These range from the lunatic fringe of those who said that he never existed, even identifying him with a sacred mushroom (really, there is no limit to the folly of scholars) to those who, at another lunatic fringe, un-man him by seeing him as the self-conscious Second Person of the Trinity in the appearance of humanity, endowed with complete knowledge, including presumably in their view quantum chromodynamics* and general relativity and whatever lies beyond (really, there is no limit to the folly of the pious).

In between, there is a bewildering variety of interpretation. Jesus seems, in his continuing influence as in his lifetime, both to resonate with men of vastly different experience and attitudes and also to elude the total grasp of any. The nineteenth-century liberals tended to see him as one of themselves. The Jesuit George Tyrell wittily said of Adolf von Harnack* that peering at the historical Jesus* down the deep well of the intervening centuries he spied his own face reflected at the bottom. Today, the revolutionary theologians of South America tend to see Jesus as the crypto-freedom fighter, a covert ally of the zealots – a thought which, in that simplistic form, can scarcely survive the remembrance of his close relationship with many tax-gatherers, those quisling collaborators of the occupying power.

The variety and conflict of these portraits is at first disturbing. Albert Schweitzer* concluded his devastating survey of the nineteenth-century life-of-Jesus movement by concluding that Jesus remains a mystery:

> He comes to us as one unknown, without a name, as of old by the lakeside he came to those men who knew him not. He speaks to us the same word: 'Follow thou me' and sets us to the tasks which he has to fulfil for our time. He commands. And to those who obey him, whether they be wise or simple, he will reveal himself in the toils, the conflicts, the sufferings which they shall pass through in his fellowship, and, as an ineffable mystery, they shall learn in their experience who he is.

Schweitzer's abandonment of his theology and musicology to labour in a remote clinic in equatorial Africa is a moving sign of the seriousness with which he took his own words. Yet, much as we must respect his actions, I believe that his attitude grossly overestimates the elusiveness of the historical Jesus. It is another of those extreme ('astronomical') reactions to the perception of a problem.

I want to try to draw attention to certain aspects of Jesus which I believe are well attested and which are of significance in assessing his contribution to our understanding of the way the world is. We shall need to consider not only his words and deeds, but also those things that were said about him by his contemporaries. If we were writing the biography of some great figure of our times, we would want not only to read his *Who's Who* entry and his speeches, but also to talk to those who had been influenced by him. It is inescapable that, in the assessment of persons, the opinions and reactions of others are part of the facts with which we have to deal.

Let us, however, begin with Jesus' deeds. One of the most certain things about him was that he was a wonder-worker. Whatever one may think about the historicity of one particular story or another, the general fact is ineradicable from the Gospels. For example, it is clear that he was in conflict with the Jewish authorities, that the question of sabbath observance was one of the most sensitive issues between them, and that Jesus gave offence by the remarkable works of healing which he performed on the day of rest (for instance, Mark 3.1-6). If Jesus did not actually do these acts of healing where was the point of the controversy?

In an earlier age, of course, the miracles would have been one of the strongest weapons in the armoury of apologetic. A man who did such things must at the very least have the power of God with him. Jesus himself is represented as using this argument when he said 'If it is by the finger of God that I cast out demons then the kingdom of God has come upon you' (Luke 11.20 par.[1]). For us today, by one of those twists that make up intellectual history, miracles are rather an embarrassment. We are so impressed by the regularity of the world that any story which is full of strange happenings acquires an air of fairy tale and invention.

Of course, some of the events which seemed inexplicable at that time may be comprehended by us today; release from hysterical paralysis, for instance. Other events, like the stilling of the storm (Mark 4.35-41 par.) may be the sort of coincidence which is fraught with significance for those present, like the long calm in the English Channel at the time of Dunkirk. I do not think that it is only repeatable occurrences which carry meaning; our whole personal experience is that there is deep significance in the unique. It is worth noting that even the most unpicturable miracles, like the feeding of the five thousand (Mark 6.34-44 par.), are recounted in a curiously matter-of-fact way, with no attempt to dwell on the marvellous details. There is a restraint about the Gospels which is very impressive when you compare them with the extravagant tone of the apocryphal gospels*,

1. = parallels, that is, there are parallel accounts in other Gospels, which you can locate with the aid of a reference Bible or book of gospel parallels. I indicate the existence of parallels to verses I quote, not as a scholarly affectation, but as an indication that comparisons can be made.

popular compositions of the second century and later which pandered to the pious imagination. Nevertheless an element of that which is contrary to common experience is inescapable in Christianity if only because it rests on the central miracle of all, the resurrection of Jesus from the dead.

The resurrection is something which will require a separate chapter (ch. 8). In the meantime, what are we to make of this miraculous element in the New Testament?

The history of science is full of the unprecedented and unexpected. Electrical conduction in metals behaves in an orderly way until suddenly, below a critical temperature, some metals lose their electrical resistance altogether and become superconducting*. Changing circumstances (in this case, lowering the temperature) have created a new regime in which physical behaviour is suddenly different. As the physicists say, a phase change has occurred. The task of the scientist faced with such a phenomenon is to try to find the underlying regularity which embraces both the old familiar regime and the strange new one revealed to him. The coherent achievement of that task is what constitutes the advance of scientific understanding. Ohm's law* is not an unbreakable law of the Medes and Persians, but it can be subsumed into a wider framework of order. In the case of superconductivity it took more than fifty years from the discovery of the phenomenon by Kammerlingh Onnes* to its explanation by Bardeen, Cooper and Schrieffer.*

It is the claim of the New Testament (see p. 57) that in Jesus a totally new regime entered the realm of human experience. If that is the case, then it is to be expected that it might be accompanied by new phenomena. The test of credibility will lie in whether one can articulate a coherent understanding of the world in which such phenomena can find a fitting place.

The problem of miracles is the problem of finding that wider framework in which they can find a coherent place. This is demanded not by science but by theology itself. 'Intervention' is not a word that one can properly use of

God in any fitful or *tour de force* sense. His relationship to his creation must be faithful and consistent if it is to be in accord with his eternal nature. I believe that the regularity of the world, which makes science possible, is a pale reflection of that. Of course, consistency does not mean superficial uniformity. The laws of physics are the same in superconducting and in ordinary regimes, though the consequences are spectacularly different. So it is that God's presence and power may be more transparently perceptible in some circumstances than in others. Nevertheless, we seek an understanding of his ways which sees him as the consisent creator and not as a celestial conjuror. I shall argue in a later chapter that it is the presence of such an embracing rationality which makes the resurrection credible.

We must now turn from Jesus' deeds to his words. Endless books have been written on the subject. I can only draw your attention to a few points which strike me forcibly when I read the Gospels.

Jesus came with a message to proclaim: the coming of the Kingdom of God. He makes his public appearance after his baptism by John, declaring, 'The time is fulfilled and the Kingdom of God is at hand; repent and believe the gospel' (Mark 1.15 par.). The Kingdom of God is not a territory, but the sovereign rule of God. Of course, Israel had always recognized that her true king was God and that he is Lord over his creation. However his rule was a hidden rule, often as hard for them to discern in the flux of the world as it is for us today. Jesus asserts that what was hidden is being made manifest, that the sovereignty of God is irrupting into the world. A new regime is coming into being.

The theme of the Kingdom is reiterated through the synoptic Gospels, as a glance at a concordance will show. (Matthew calls it the Kingdom of Heaven, using a customary Jewish periphrasis for God. Jews had so high a view of God's majesty that they were reluctant to make explicit reference to the deity. The divine name itself, the tetragrammaton YHWH*, was only uttered by the High Priest alone, once a year on the day of atonement.) It is the subject of many of Jesus' parables: the mustard seed (Mark 4.30–32 par.); the hidden treasure (Matt. 13.44); the pearl of great price (Matt. 13.45); and many more. These parables make it clear that the Kingdom is of great value and that its imminence calls for decisive action. (That is the point, presumably, of the otherwise rather unedifying story of the unjust steward (Luke 16.1–8), who, on being threatened with dismissal, acted quickly to use his master's goods to obtain the friendship of those who could help him when he lost his job.) There is a note of promise and of urgency in the air.

When we consider the sort of claims Jesus made about himself, we find this note of decision and crisis is sustained. The synoptic Gospels portray a considerable reticence on his part. In all of them a climax is reached at Caesarea Philippi when, in reply to Jesus' questioning, Peter makes his celebrated confession 'You are the Christ' – that is, the anointed one (Hebrew: Messiah*) who was the expected instrument of God's rule (Mark 8.27–30 par.). Rather than encouraging Peter and the disciples to spread the news, we read that Jesus 'charged them to tell no one about him'. Partly, no doubt, this was because of the ambivalence of the concept of a Messiah in a politically sensitive Palestine where the Jews longed for a military deliverer to rid them of the Roman yoke. Jesus' entry into Jerusalem riding on a donkey rather than a war horse was a deliberate sign of his repudiation of that role. Partly, however, it may have been due to his unwillingness to accept the type-casting of any specific title.

Yet there is one title that he does seem to have taken openly to himself, the mysterious phrase 'The Son of Man'.* In saying that, I have to admit that I am making a claim with which not all scholars would agree. We are back in that 'astronomical' area of debate where limited data and unlimited human ingenuity can produce a number of answers of varying plausibility. (Are strongly red-shifted quasars immensely bright and distant objects

57

or something peculiar which is nearer by?) What is beyond dispute is that all four Gospels repeatedly portray Jesus as using the phrase 'The Son of Man'; that it is never applied to any other contemporary figure; and that, with the exception of the words of Stephen (Acts 7.56), it is never even used by anyone other than Jesus himself. These are very striking facts and I cannot see that they have a likely explanation other than that in this phrase we have the title which was Jesus' own choice.

'Son of Man' is as grotesquely odd a phrase in Greek as it is in English (another reason for supposing it unlikely to be a later invention). In Aramaic and in Hebrew, however, it is quite a natural turn of phrase and its meaning generally is just equivalent to that of 'man', *simpliciter*. In the book of Ezekiel the prophet is continually addressed by God as 'Son of Man', and there seems no reason to suppose that it carries any unusual significance in that case. Although Jesus may occasionally use it in this undifferentiated way it would make nonsense of his sayings if one simply turned 'Son of Man' into 'man' throughout. What then is its special significance on his lips?

There are two possible places from which clues might be obtained. (Notice that Jesus never offers any explanation of the phrase himself, nor do the evangelists feel the need to add an explanatory gloss.) One source is a weird book of more or less the first-century period, called the *Book of Enoch*, one of the many apocalyptic writings, ostensibly purporting to originate from Old Testament characters, which circulated among the Jews at that time. It has passages in which 'Son of Man' is used with a clearly messianic meaning. However, *Enoch* as we know it is a mishmash of different sources and it is quite possible that the Son of Man passages are later interpolations by Christians seeking to improve on the original. Much more to the point – and in its way nearly as strange – is the very late (second century BC) Old Testament book of Daniel. In Chapter 7 we read of a mysterious vision:

And behold, with the clouds of heaven there came one like a son of man and he came to the Ancient of Days [that is, God] and was presented before him and to him was given dominion and glory and kingdom, that all peoples, nations and languages should serve him; his dominion is an everlasting dominion which shall not pass away and his kingdom one that shall not be destroyed. (Dan. 7.13–14)

The words spoken by Jesus at his trial before the High Priest, 'You will see the Son of Man seated at the right hand of Power and coming with the clouds of heaven' (Mark 14.62 par.) are a clear echo of Daniel 7.

The way in which Jesus used the phrase, 'the Son of Man' is odd, for there are two different ways in which he did so. At times he is indisputably referring to himself: 'The Son of Man came eating and drinking and they say "Behold, a glutton and a drunkard, a friend of tax collectors and sinners"' (Matt. 11.19 par.). At other times there is reference to a figure who will appear at the final denouement of all things, who is related to Jesus but not clearly identified with him: 'For whoever is ashamed of me and of my words in this adulterous and sinful generation, of him will the Son of Man also be ashamed when he comes in the glory of his Father with the holy angels' (Mark 8.38 par.).

Perhaps the reason Jesus used the title of the Son of Man was that it had this elusive flexibility, a mysterious openness to that great future act of God in which his sovereignty would be unequivocally manifested and with which Jesus was in some way uniquely to be associated. We are back to the promise and urgency of the coming Kingdom. There is in the words of Jesus (and in the New Testament generally) a strongly eschatological* note, that is a concern with some final act of God in which what has been hidden and implicit in this present age will be made overt and explicit in a new age in which God's righteousness and power will be manifestly vindicated over the apparent ambivalence of our present experience.

These are high hopes, and we shall have to ask what became of them. The end of Jesus' life is the enigma which puts the question. Schweitzer believed that Jesus sought his own death as a lever to activate the eschatological purpose of God:

> Jesus . . . in the knowledge that he is the coming Son of Man lays hold of the wheel of the world to set it moving on that last revolution which is to bring all ordinary history to a close. It refuses to turn, and he throws himself upon it. Then it does turn and it crushes him. Instead of bringing in the eschatological conditions, he has destroyed them. The wheel rolls onward, and the mangled body of the one immeasurably great man, who was strong enough to think of himself as the spiritual ruler of mankind and to bend history to his purpose, is hanging upon it still. That is his victory and his reign.

The rhetoric is magnificent, but is it true? The picture is one of heroic delusion, of hubris, the attempt to force the hand of God. I believe that the truth is more tragic, more hopeful and more profound than that. We shall have to consider the question in succeeding chapters.

Jesus' words contain implicit claims as well as explicit. They can be summed up in two Aramaic words, so characteristic of his speech that they are left untranslated in the Greek of the New Testament: *amen* (truly, so be it) and *abba* (father).

We are familiar with 'amen' at the end of a prayer as a mark of concurrence with what has been said. This usage would also have been natural for the people of Jesus' day (see, for example, the endings of several of Paul's epistles, Rom. 16.27, etc.). Jesus, however, employs the word completely differently, for he puts it at the beginning. His characteristic phrase is 'Amen, I say to you . . .' which appears forty-nine times in the synoptics (in many English versions its appearance is disguised by its being translated 'truly' or 'verily') or the Johannine version 'Amen, amen, I say to you . . .' which appears twenty-four times in the fourth Gospel. This way of using amen is idiosyncratic to Jesus; no one else is ever represented as using it. Thus there can be no doubt that in it we hear his original voice. Its force is considerable, for it is an unequivocal assertion that what follows in Jesus' pronouncement is certainly the case. Here is no rabbi engaged in the characteristic Jewish pleasure of argumentative discussion. He is the one who knows. We are not surprised that people 'were astonished at his teaching for he taught as one who had authority and not as the scribes' (Mark 1.22 par.).

And what sort of things did he have to say? Look at Matthew 5, part of the Sermon on the Mount. There are six passages, each beginning 'You have heard that it was said [to the men of old] . . . but *I* say to you . . .', in which Jesus deepens or corrects Old Testament moral teaching. What is this business about it having been said to men of old? Jesus is not referring to some learned scribal discussion of the past. He is taking precepts of the *torah*,* the law that was the very foundation of Jewish religion, revealed by God to Moses on the holy mountain of Sinai. A man who sets out to put the *torah* right is making very substantial claims indeed for himself.

A pious Jew of the first century would be familiar with the idea of the fatherhood of God. However, it is a different matter when in Mark 14.36 Jesus, praying in agony in the garden of Gethsemane, addresses God with the single word 'Abba', a word of such family intimacy that it might almost be rendered 'Daddy'. One has the feeling that the Aramaic has been preserved to soften the shock of such familiarity with a God otherwise conceived of as so lofty that his name, YHWH, might be uttered only once a year and that by the High Priest alone. (Matt. 26.39 and Luke 22.42 both tone Mark down.) That single word 'abba' contains in implicit miniature the sort of intimate relationship with God claimed explicitly in the words of the Johannine Christ. Jesus' followers felt that they too had been admitted to the intimacy of children of God through him. Paul speaks of us being able in the

61

Spirit to cry 'Abba, father' (Rom. 8.15, Gal. 4.6). It is highly probable that the original Aramaic version of the Lord's prayer began 'Abba'. (Compare the 'Father' of Luke 11.2 with the characteristically more respectful 'Our Father' of Matthew 6.9.) Scholars tell us that this degree of family intimacy with God is a feature of Jesus' teaching which is wholly without parallel in contemporary Judaism.

So much for Jesus' own attitude. What about the impression he made upon his immediate followers? A full answer would call for an extensive survey of New Testament material. I must content myself with three pointers which I believe are a fair sample of the evidence available.

As was customary at the time, Paul opens his letters with a greeting to his readers. A favourite form for him includes the phrase 'Grace to you and peace from God our Father and the Lord Jesus Christ' (Rom. 1.7, 1 Cor. 1.3, etc.). Two things strike one about that phrase. The first is the juxtaposition of God and Jesus. Paul can place them in tandem without any feeling of incongruity or impropriety. It would be absurdly bathetic to couple together 'God and Paul', or even 'God and Moses', but for Jesus it seems that this is not so. He is fit, so to speak, to stand in such august company. Remember that the writer is one who had grown up in the fiercely monotheistic faith of Israel and you will see that this is a very significant fact.

Yet the second thing that strikes one is that Paul does not identify God and Jesus. A later Christian writer might well have wished to begin 'In the name of the Triune God, Father, Son and Holy Spirit'. We do not find that sort of language in the New Testament (but notice its incipience in the celebrated verse of 2 Cor. 13.14: 'The grace of the Lord Jesus Christ, the love of God and the fellowship of the Holy Spirit be with you all').

Jesus is called 'Lord' in Paul's greeting and my second point is to consider the implications of this. The corresponding Greek work *kyrios* is an interesting one. In the vocative, *kyrie*, it need mean no more than a greeting of respect, just as our calling someone 'sir' does not carry the implication that he has received the accolade of knighthood. Outside that usage, however, it is a loaded word. We have noticed how reverently the Jews regarded the divine name YHWH, and how scrupulously they refrained from uttering it. This presented a problem in reading aloud the Scriptures in which the divine name naturally frequently occurs. The problem was solved by the pious Jew saying instead the word '*adonai*', the Hebrew for Lord. When the Greek-speaking Jews of Alexandria made their translation of the Old Testament in the third century BC, they wrote *kyrios* everywhere that the Hebrew text read YHWH. (Much the same thing happens in a number of English versions where LORD is written for the divine name.) Consequently we can see that *kyrios* is not the sort of title which Jews would use in a thoughtless way. It is charged with a special significance. The implications of this appear with startling clarity when we find Paul in Romans 10.13 quoting the words of the Old Testament prophet Joel: 'Everyone who calls on the name of the Lord will be saved'. Of course, the prophet meant YHWH, the God of Israel. Paul is applying these words to Jesus.

Was that just the sort of dangerous twist that Paul gave to Christianity, the kind of distortion which some people have thought that Paul introduced, turning the simple piety of Jesus into a theologically complicated Saviour-cult? The evidence we have points to the contrary. Not only is such a view inadequate to account for the strange claims we have found in the words of Jesus himself, but it also fails to reckon with the indications that the very earliest Christian confession appears to have been 'Jesus is Lord'. Earlier in the same chapter of Romans Paul recalls to his readers that 'If you confess with your lips that Jesus is Lord and believe in your heart that God raised him from the dead you will be saved' (Rom. 10.9). He is writing to a church which he did not found and which he had not even at that time visited. Yet the confession 'Jesus is Lord' appears to be such common Christian currency that he can appeal to it (see also 1 Cor. 12.3, Phil. 2.11). The Book of Acts has Peter telling his hearers on the day of Pentecost that they may 'know assuredly that God has made him both Lord and Christ, this Jesus whom you crucified' (Acts 2.36).

All the writers of the New Testament regard Jesus, not as an inspiring figure of the immediate past but as a living Lord in the active present. In Paul we find a further element which is even more difficult for the modern mind to grasp. My third point is the curiously corporate aspect to the understanding of the post-resurrection Christ which we find in some parts of the New Testament. 'As in Adam all die, even so in Christ shall all be made alive' (1 Cor. 15.22). The first part of this sentence we must surely incline to see as a picturesquely mythological way of expressing the fact that death comes to all men. Is not the second then just an equally picturesque and mythological way of saying that the Christian hope is of resurrection for all men? It is a bit odd, however, to use as a mythological archetype, not a shadowy figure of the distant past, but someone who was alive within living memory. Moreover, this sort of language recurs. 'If anyone is in Christ he is a new creation, the old has passed away, behold the new is come' (2 Cor. 5.17). This seems a bit overdone if it is simply conveying the notion that the example of Jesus will help us turn over (yet another?) moral new leaf. This manner of speaking finds its climax in the statement that Christians constitute the body of Christ: 'You are the body of Christ and individually members of it' (v.27 from the long passage 1 Cor. 12.4–31; see also Rom. 12.3–8, Eph. 5.23–33).

That sort of talk could not be farther from what has immediate appeal and comprehensibility to most of us today. Some of my readers may well feel impatience, or even embarrassment, at it. I can only repeat what I said earlier (p. 50), that I feel that we do well not to be over-hasty in rejecting the insights of other ages into a degree of human solidarity – strange though that thought certainly is in the private world of twentieth-century men. I shall have to return to this point once more, and in greater detail, in the next chapter.

Meanwhile, note that this sort of corporate discussion, though not omnipresent in the New Testament, is not confined to Paul alone. That other great theological genius, the author of the fourth Gospel, whose style and attitude is in so many ways different from Paul's, says very much the same thing in his own particular way: 'Abide in me and I in you . . . I am the vine, you are the branches' (John 15.4–5). It may also be that the characteristic 'the Son of Man' of Jesus' own utterance carried a corporate overtone. A few verses later in the chapter of Daniel from which I quoted earlier, we are given an interpretation of the dreams that Daniel has had. It includes the statement 'The saints of the Most High shall receive the kingdom and possess the kingdom for ever and ever' (Dan. 7.18). Although it is not specifically stated that the saints of the Most High (that is, Jews who had suffered grievous persecution under the Seleucid* king Antiochus Epiphanes) are to be identified with the figure like a son of man in the dream, it seems natural to do so. In that case the phrase the Son of Man would be capable of taking a curiously corporate reference also.

What are we to make of it all? A great deal depends upon our assessment of the strange end to Jesus' life which we shall consider in the next two chapters. An important factor which will emerge is the New Testament conviction that those three days from Good Friday to Easter Sunday encompass a great act of God in Jesus by which human destiny is permanently affected. This is what theologians call the Work of Christ. If we come to believe that this view is correct it carries astonishing implications about who he must have been for this to be so. Nevertheless the credibility of such a claim must in part rest on who Jesus appeared to be outside that critical three-day period: the words and deeds of the man who was crucified; the aftermath in the lives of those who persisted as his followers after his ignominious death.

We must now try to draw some of the threads of this chapter together. It is not an easy task. Jesus did not say 'I am God' (what sane man could?). Very seldom indeed does anyone in the New Testament say categorically 'He was God' (one rare example from the fourth Gospel is the previously doubting Thomas's confession 'My Lord and my God' (John 20.28); but notice that it is the risen Christ and not the earthly Jesus who is thus addressed). Yet in Jesus' words and in the reactions of his followers to him we have seen a persistent and implicit element of testimony to the divine at work to a degree which seems inadequately described by simply saying that he was an inspired man, the greatest of the prophets. Both in the pregnantly allusive reticence of Jesus and in the unresolved ambiguities of Paul ('God our Father and the Lord Jesus Christ') and John ('I and the Father are one'; 'My Father is greater than I') we have the impression of something present which transcends what has been articulated. It is as though men are struggling to come to terms with a phenomenon so remarkable and unique that, though they hesitate to say that in a man God was present, yet they can find no point of satisfactory understanding which falls short of that paradoxical claim.

This wrestling with the phenomenon of Jesus continued in the post-New Testament Church and, of course, within its mainstream it led to the doctrine of the incarnation, that in Jesus God himself had taken a role on the stage of his creation.

Is such a thought credible? Of course it carries with it grave difficulties of understanding. How can the divine be present in a man without completely overwhelming and obliterating his humanity? It calls for the projection of infinite dimensions on to a finite dimensional image. How can a man, born into the nexus of flawed humanity, so escape its consequences as to be the focused image of the holy God? It is a popular modern phrase to speak of

Jesus as a 'window into God'. Would not any human 'window' be so refracting as to distort the divine out of recognition? And if it does not, in what sense is it recognizably human?

Such questions are to be considered, not in terms of a priori argument, but by trying to see the way that things are. For me, though Jesus is obviously a man, there is in him an element to which I cannot refrain from attributing the character of the divine. Like Thomas I have to say 'My Lord and my God'. At the rational level, I am led to that confession partly by the considerations of this chapter, and partly by those of the chapters to come. I do not purport to understand how this can be, but I know that I cannot deny it. A lesser view of Jesus would be easier to comprehend but it would be inadequate to the phenomenon.

One cannot write about the two natures of Christ (as theologians call the mingling of human and divine in Jesus) without being irresistibly reminded of the wave/particle duality of light described on page 25. How can something be both a wave and a particle? The physicists of the early years of this century did not know. They had simply experienced that that was the way it was, and they had to live with it. Of course physics found eventual understanding in the beautiful work of Paul Dirac when he created the first example of a quantum field theory. Christology has not yet found its Dirac. Perhaps it never will.

In physics we deal with matter which is at our disposal to interrogate as we please. Therein lies the power of the experimental method and the source of the great success of science. People are different. They cannot be manipulated. Even less can God be manipulated. 'You shall not put the Lord your God to the test' (Deut. 6.16) is an inescapable part of our experience of him. At times this leads to an understandable impatience on the part of those who stand outside the community of faith (and even those within it). A child is ill and the Church prays for his recovery. If the child lives the Church rejoices that that was the will of God. But if the child dies, the Church in its sorrow seeks to accept that as the will of God also. Is God's head never on the block? Is it always heads he wins, tails you lose? I am afraid that some degree of inscrutability will always be part of the mystery of God. There is a strong element within theology of what is known as the apophatic tradition,* the recognition that God's otherness puts him beyond our finite grasp. Such a consideration is not to be used as an excuse for mental laziness or sloppy thinking, but it does set limits to the extent to which the theological enterprise can expect to achieve complete success.

SEVEN

The Death of Jesus

Consider these two accounts, each telling of a man's death imposed by the state:

> He said to the jailer 'You my good friend, who are experienced in these matters shall give me directions how I am to proceed'. The man answered 'You have only to walk about until your legs are heavy, and then lie down and the poison will act'. Then raising the cup to his lips, quite readily and cheerfully he drank off the poison. As the bystanders wept he said 'What is this strange outcry? Be quiet and have patience'. He said 'When the poison reaches the heart, that will be the end'. He was beginning to grow cold about the groin when he uncovered his face and said 'I owe a cock to Asclepius; will you remember to pay the debt?' 'The debt shall be paid' a bystander said. In a minute or two a movement was heard and the attendants uncovered him; his eyes were set. Such was his end.

> He began to be greatly distressed and troubled and he said to his friends 'My soul is very sorrowful even to death; remain here and watch'. He said 'Father, all things are possible to thee, remove this cup from me; yet not what I will but what thou wilt' . . . They led him out to crucify him. And when the sixth hour had come there was darkness over the whole land until the ninth hour. And at the ninth hour he cried with a loud voice 'My God, my God, why hast thou forsaken me?'. And he uttered a loud cry and breathed his last.

The first is the death of Socrates, condensed from Plato's

Phaedo. The second is the death of Jesus, condensed from Mark's Gospel. The contrast is very great. Socrates, after a preceding discourse in which he establishes to his own satisfaction the doctrine of the immortality of the soul, meets his death with a calm serenity. The death of Jesus, however, is preceded by the agony of reluctance in the garden of Gethsemane and it is consummated in a time of darkness pierced by a terrible cry of dereliction.

Of course the ways in which the two deaths were procured were very different. Socrates died a civilized death brought about by drinking hemlock. Jesus suffered the cruel Roman punishment of execution by crucifixion. We are so used to that bland representation of the man on the cross which constitutes the average crucifix that we forget how degrading a death it was – the pain of the wounds, the heat of the sun, the agony of breathing, the shame of public exposure in circumstances when bodily functions would be beyond control, the long-drawn out struggle to die. The twisted figure of Grünewald's Isenheim altarpiece, or the macabre crucifixes of South America (a continent which understands violent death) are much nearer a true account. Yet this by itself cannot explain the differences between the two executions. Many of Jesus' followers subsequently faced deaths of equal pain and shame, but with a marvellous fortitude and with the praises of God on their lips. There is a deeper mystery at work in that desolate figure on the cross.

The Gospels attach the greatest importance to the death of Jesus. Six of Mark's sixteen chapters are devoted to that last week in Jerusalem, the story of the crucifixion, its prelude and its aftermath. The narrative has a continuity which contrasts with the bitty character of the collections of pericopes which precede it. In that thirty-five-year period in which traditions circulated before the first Gospel was composed it seems clear that a coherent passion narrative must have come early into being. The accounts in the other three Gospels are equally extensive.

There are, of course, differences of detail between the evangelists over which scholars rightly puzzle, particularly in the accounts of the trials which Jesus was forced hastily to undergo. There is a celebrated contradiction between John and the synoptics about the dating of the crucifixion. All agree that it was on a Friday, but the synoptists say that it was the passover day whilst John asserts it to have been the day of preparation preceding the passover. (It is possible that a theological nuance has affected John's statement on the matter – the day of preparation was the day on which the passover lambs were slain in the Temple.) For our present purpose it is not necessary to pursue these matters in detail. In its essential character the evangelists all tell the same story. Jesus died, betrayed by Judas, deserted by his friends, rejected by the nation of Israel to whom he came. In darkness and in isolation even from God his Father, he uttered that not very brave cry 'My God, my God, why hast thou forsaken me?'. I do not think that the effect of that terrible cry is softened by noting that it is the first line of Psalm 22. Mark and Matthew both record the cry of dereliction, giving the original Aramaic 'Eloi, Eloi, lama sabachthani?' as an awesome record of what had come to pass. Luke, whose account of the passion is the most serene, omits it. John, with characteristic ironic understatement has his own equivalent. In his Gospel Jesus says 'I thirst' (John 19.28). We realize the force of that when we recall that this is the man who told the woman of Samaria that whoever drank of the water which he would give would never thirst (John 4.14) and who had stood up and proclaimed in the Temple 'If anyone thirst let him come to me and drink' (John 7.38). John perceives in the death of Jesus a reversal of his life as total as that recorded by the synoptics.

What are we to make of it all? What has become of all those high hopes of the coming of the Kingdom of God? Does it all end in a lonely cry in the dark, a good man snuffed out by the contrariness of human life? Jesus may have taught with authority but has the final turning of the wheel of the world crushed it out of him?

It is a remarkable fact that the writers of the New

Testament do not see it that way. In that lonely figure in the dark, in the spent force of a deserted man dying on a cross, they see not the ultimate triumph of evil or futility but the only source of hope for mankind. Let Paul speak for them all. Writing to the Corinthians he said that in the cross we see that 'God was in Christ reconciling the world to himself' (2 Cor. 5.19). Such a thought is deeply mysterious, beyond our power to grasp in its entirety, but since it points to the heart of the Christian understanding of the way the world is we must make whatever shift we can to gain some insight into it.

'God was in Christ.' The crucifixion was not something which got dreadfully out of hand, a tragic mistake which marred an otherwise wonderful life. On the contrary, it was the inevitable fulfilment of the life, purposed by God. Jesus deliberately set out for Jerusalem on that final expedition, when he could have stayed in the comparative safety of Galilee. Mark tells us that he strode ahead with his disciples following 'amazed and afraid' (Mark 10.32). They could see what was to come. The synoptists say that three times Jesus predicted his coming death (Mark 8.31, 9.31, 10.33–34, par.). Scholars have argued about these predictions, whether Jesus uttered them or whether they are predictions after the event inserted by the early Church. Certainly some of the detail may be retrojected from the form that the passion actually took, but there is nothing improbable in Jesus' perceiving that an encounter with the hostile authorities was going to cost him his life. Whatever the agony in the garden of Gethsemane means (and we shall have to return to that) it did not arise from a sudden realization by Jesus for the first time that he was past the point of no return. That had been accepted much earlier. God's hand was seen at work in these events. The Book of Acts has Peter telling the Jerusalem crowd on the day of Pentecost that Jesus was 'delivered up according to the definite plan and foreknowledge of God' (Acts 2.23).

However, the meaning of 'God was in Christ' lies much

deeper than the simple assertion that in the cross we see an act of suffering freely embraced by the sufferer as his acceptance of the mysterious purpose of God. What we are asked to consider is that in that totally isolated, totally helpless, figure hanging on the cross, we see God himself caught up and impaled on the contradictions of the strange world he has made. The Christian God is not a detached if compassionate beholder of the sufferings of the world, he is a participant in them. It is the crucified God whom we worship.

E. Weisel, a Jewish survivor of Auschwitz, tells in his book *Night* this story:

> The SS hanged two Jewish men and a youth in front of the whole camp. The men died quickly but the death throes of the youth lasted for half an hour. 'Where is God? Where is he?' someone asked behind me. As the youth still hung in torment in the noose after a long time I heard the man call again 'Where is God now?'. And I heard a voice in myself answer: 'Where is he? He is here. He is hanging there on the gallows . . .'

The intense suffering of the concentration camp had revealed a profound truth. On the gallows of Calvary God's head was caught in the noose and the rope drawn tight.

This strange thought provides some glimmer of light in the darkness of human suffering. It does not explain away pain and evil but it meets them on a level commensurate with the agonizing problem that they pose. Ultimately in these deep matters it is not so much what is said but the tone in which it is said which counts. C. S. Lewis wrote two books about suffering. One was *The Problem of Pain*, characteristically acute and well argued, but in its urbane donnish phrases remote from the centre of suffering. The other was *A Grief Observed*. First published pseudonymously, it told of his experience as his wife Joy, whom he had married as a quixotic gesture of help but with whom he had found unexpected happiness, died slowly of cancer. This second book offers no explanation of the meaning of such a fate but, written from the heart, it speaks to the heart. The Christian assertion is that the heart at the centre of reality is revealed in the pinioned arms and twisted body of the man hanging on the tree.

'God was . . . reconciling the world to himself.' The cross appears to be the epitome of weakness. What is more helpless than a man nailed to a tree and left to die? It is the witness of the New Testament that, by the strange alchemy of God, that act of weakness is the source of power from which comes all human hope.

There is a flawed character to our existence. Earlier (p. 20) we considered the entail of lovelessness in which we are all caught up. Promise is never quite fulfilled. Bright youth becomes wary middle age; the liberator of his country proves its next tyrant. The poignance of children lies in the contemplation of their innocence which will so soon be dusted over by 'realism'. We thrill to the words 'love bears all things, believes all things, hopes all things' (1 Cor. 13.7) but cannot stand the boringly reiterated reminiscences of our elderly neighbour.

If Jesus just came to give us good advice, even better advice than had ever been given before, he was merely adding to an already large stock, much of which proves unusable. It is not advice that we need but a transforming power to enable us to follow it. That is why words like Paul's 'If any man be in Christ he is a new creation' (2 Cor. 5.17) seem to speak with such an incredible promise.

The Christian understanding of the flawed character of our human nature is that it arises from an alienation from the true ground of our being, an alienation from God. He alone is the true source of love and healing and power. We are not destined to self-complete autonomy, but it is in his service alone that we find our perfect freedom and fulfilment. The source of this alienation is unknown; the myth of the Fall is more the record of the fact than the explanation of its origin.

It is also the Christian understanding that the cross of

Christ is the point of reconciliation, the way by which men can find their way back to God. Now this is a very strange thought. How can the death of one man, far away and long ago, have any effect on me today, except perhaps as a touching example of the acceptance of unmerited suffering? Why is the death of this first-century Jew of greater significance than that of the millions of his fellow Jews who were sent to unprotesting innocent deaths in the holocaust of our century?

Perhaps the first thing to notice is the fact that from the very first the death of Jesus was perceived as having this transcending significance. That is why the passion narrative formed so early in the tradition. People were so caught by their experience of liberation through his death that it was centuries before they began to ask the question, so natural to us, of how this could be. While the Greek fathers exercised the subtlety of their minds on the mysteries of the Trinity and of the two natures of Christ, the experience of salvation* through the cross was not put to the same degree of analysis. It was as though the facts were too well known to need explanation. (It took a clever man like Olbers* to ask why the sky was dark at night.)

When explanations of the saving death of Christ were sought for, the first ones propounded were of a manifestly crude and unsatisfactory character. Often theology had little better to offer than the 'deceiver-deceived' – the devil accepted the man Jesus as the payment for sin, not realizing that he was also divine and would thus escape from his clutches. It is deeply humiliating to have to summarize so unworthy a proposal.

I have emphasized this because I think it is important to recognize that things can be true, and manifest themselves as true, without our necessarily being in possession of a theoretical understanding of them. (I do not need to know microelectronics before I can use my pocket calculator.) Nevertheless it is inevitable and right that we should seek to attain such a degree of comprehension as lies within our grasp.

For me an understanding (of course partial and groping) of the work of Christ on the cross centres on two things: the fact that in Jesus elements of both the human and the divine intermingle, and the fact of human solidarity.

The problem at issue is the overcoming of human alienation from God, the breaking of the entail of lovelessness. Because it is a human problem, human nature must be totally involved. It was a very important insight, which the Greek fathers did achieve when they said that 'what is not assumed is not redeemed'. Jesus had to be fully human and to enter into a truly human experience if he was to be of any relevance to us at all. That, I believe, is the reason for the agony of Gethsemane and the dereliction of the cross. It is part of the human experience to dread the approach of death. It is part of the human experience to have moments when we feel deserted by God, alone in a hostile world. All that experience had, so to speak, to partake in the act of redemption. However, because what was sought was release from our alienation from God, God also had to participate in the deed. It was *God* who was in Christ, reconciling the world to himself. Only in the God-man Jesus could human need and divine power find a meeting point.

They may meet there, but how do we find our lodgement there also? To put it bluntly, Jesus may have died for himself; how could he have died for me? If we are all totally separate from each other, living lives of insulated independence, I think it is very hard to see how that question finds an answer. But, however strange it may seem to twentieth-century man to say so, I do not think that the strictly individualistic model is the correct picture of mankind. If there is a deep level at which human solidarity prevails, then it can be the case, as the writer to the Hebrews says, that Jesus is 'the pioneer of our salvation' (Heb. 2.10), for at that level we are joined to him.

Why is the culminating act of reconciliation a death? Why was not Jesus' life sufficient to reconcile us to God? Reconciliation involves forgiveness for the effects of the alienating forces which have been at work (for sin,* as Christians say). We know something of forgiveness in our daily lives. It is a costly business. It is not enough for forgiver or forgiven to pretend that it did not matter. It did matter. The hurt was real; some of the consequences may be lasting. The digestion of that hurt and the acceptance of those consequences are the cost of forgiveness. That cost is not a punishment in which the forgiver exacts a shameful remorse from the one forgiven. It is a cost in which both share. It is hard to forgive a real wrong; it is hard to accept the real forgiveness of a wrong. I think that this costliness of forgiveness is the clue to why the act of redemption had to involve the total surrender of death. 'In this is love, not that we loved God but that he loved us and sent his son to be the expiation for our sins' (1 John 4.10). 'God shows his love towards us in that while we were yet sinners Christ died for us' (Rom. 5.8).

If it is true that in the weakness and dereliction of the cross lies the powerful act of God for our redemption and the pledge of his love for us, then we begin to see that the death of Jesus was not the marring of his life but the fulfilment of it. The enigma finds an answer. Jesus spoke of the coming of the Kingdom of God, the irruption of God's manifest sovereignty into the world. Precisely at that moment when all seemed lost, that Kingdom in fact came. The Christian paradox speaks of the king who reigns from the gallows. No one saw this more clearly than the author of the fourth Gospel. For John the moment of deepest darkness is the moment of true glory. Jesus says ' "Now is the judgement of this world, now shall the ruler of this world be cast out; and I, when I am lifted up from the earth, will draw all men to myself". He said this to show what death he was to die' (John 12.31–33).

EIGHT

The Resurrection

I have been describing the death of Jesus as the first Christians understood it and as the Church has regarded it in its experience down the ages. The question is, Have they got it right? The cross is an ambiguous event. By no means all of Jesus' contemporaries saw it in the same way as the disciples.

A lonely figure dies on the tree with a cry of dereliction on his lips. A good man eventually subject to paranoiac delusion and defeat? One of the many well-intentioned who in the end found that they could not beat the system? The saviour of the world? These questions demand an answer that only God can give. Christians believe that he gave that answer by raising Jesus from the dead.

In considering the resurrection we encounter a severe problem. It is common ground that we are discussing a unique event. There are stories of people in the ancient world being restored to life. The New Testament contains several, of which the raising of Lazarus by Jesus (John 12) is the best known. These are not resurrections but resuscitations. Without question those so restored were destined eventually to die again. Among some of the Jews, but not all (see the Sadducees in Mark 12.18 par.), there was an expectation that at the end of time there would be a resurrection of all the dead.[1] This, however, was to occur as part of that great final act in which God

1. This was a very late development in Judaism, scarcely represented in the Old Testament. The latter's predominant attitude is the bleak 'Man is like the beasts that perish' (Ps. 49.12), in striking contrast with the obsession with the after-life displayed by the neighbouring Egyptian civilization.

visibly vindicated his righteousness. It was to be a universal and an eschatological event. There was absolutely no expectation that a single man would, in the middle of the course of history, be raised from the dead to die no more. Therefore, a priori, the notion of Jesus' resurrection was as strange in the first century as it is for us today. For all of us, if it is an event at all it is an event *sui generis*. The problem is, how can one begin to discuss the likelihood of the totally one-off?

The resurrection is an event which is alleged to have happened to the man Jesus, who is an historical figure. If it occurred, it must have left traces in history. We must shortly turn our attention to an assessment of the evidence for that. The investigation of that evidence may also help us to form some view of the character of the event itself. In its idiosyncratic nature it is clearly trans-historical – in the sense that history deals with the stuff of common experience and we are here concerned with an event without parallel – but that does not mean that it is wholly beyond conception. If it were it could hold no meaning for us.

An inquiry into the evidence can carry us only so far. It can demonstrate (as I believe it does) that the Christian belief in the resurrection of Jesus is not without substantial motivation, so that it is far from being an ungrounded speculation. However, at best such an inquiry can point only to a balance of probability. In an event so contrary to normal expectation as the resurrection, the way in which that balance is weighed must depend upon non-historical factors. No one can gainsay the determined sceptic like David Hume,* for whom no explanation is so implausible as that which asserts that a man rose from the dead. Equally no one need adopt so intransigent a position. Ultimately one's attitude to the resurrection will depend upon the degree to which it does or does not cohere with one's general understanding of the way the world is. If the Christian understanding is true, that in Jesus the divine and human so mingled that a new regime was present in the world, then the unique occurrence of the resurrection is conceivable, indeed probable, within that framework. If a humanist understanding is true, that Jesus was a remarkable and inspiring man but no more, then it is to be expected that death had the degree of finality for him that it will have for us.

Either argument tends to be circular, for the probabilities depend upon the interpretation, which itself is influenced by what actually happened. Both arguments contain the sort of interplay between fact and interpretation which is also characteristic of the dialogue between experiment and theory in science. Our evaluation of Jesus can no more be reduced simply to historical assessment than science can be identified with mere data (the fallacy of induction.*) On the other hand, Christianity, by focusing its understanding of the world on a particular man, can no more be independent of history than a theoretical physicist can neglect the findings of his experimental colleagues. Some Christians have felt that this makes faith intolerably contingent upon history. I welcome that contingency.

A consideration of the historical evidence for the resurrection is bound to begin with 1 Cor. 15.3–8. I have already quoted this passage in full but it is so important that it merits repetition:

> For I delivered to you as of first importance what I also received, that Christ died for our sins in accordance with the scriptures, that he was buried, that he was raised on the third day in accordance with the scriptures, and that he appeared to Cephas, then to the twelve. Then he appeared to more than five hundred brethren at one time, most of whom are still alive, though some have fallen asleep. Then he appeared to James, then to all the apostles. Last of all, as to one untimely born, he appeared to me.

In this letter written in the middle fifties of the first century (the crucifixion was about AD 30), Paul is recalling to the Corinthians the testimony he had himself received from others, presumably a short time after his conversion. We are in touch here with a tradition going back to within a very few years of the events themselves. Scholars find within the statement confirmation of its antiquity, for example in the use of 'the Twelve' to denote the inner group of Jesus' disciples, an archaic usage which soon went out of fashion in the primitive Church. Paul and the tradition are content with a bare statement that Jesus 'was raised' (note the passive; it is an act of God) and a spare listing of witnesses to his appearances, beginning with Cephas (=Peter) and ending with Paul's own Damascus road experience.

The phrase 'on the third day in accordance with the scriptures' poses a conundrum. First of all, does the reference to the scriptures qualify the third day or the raising itself? It is not easy to find specific verses of the Old Testament which might be thought to meet either point, except perhaps Psalm 16.10. 'Thou wilt not abandon my soul to Hades nor let thy Holy One see corruption' (see Acts 2.22–32), coupled with the first-century idea that corruption set in on the fourth day after death. Personally I think that the reference to the scriptures is a general one indicating that the purposes of God were at work in the resurrection of Jesus, and that the third day is an actual historical reminiscence. (I return to this later.)

It seems clear that Paul's citation of the tradition is intended to carry evidential value. The reference to the more than five hundred brethren 'most of whom are still alive' must surely make that point. And when you come to think of it, a pretty telling point it was. He is not talking about something which occurred in the shadowy past. There is an appeal to living (and presumably accessible) testimony.

If we want to seek more information about these appearances of the risen Christ we have to turn to the Gospels. At once we enter a strange dream-like realm in which Jesus appears in rooms with locked doors, disappears at will and is found hard to recognize, although those whose eyes are opened can perceive that it is the Lord. (Note, however, Matthew 28.17 where we are told with disarming honesty that 'some doubted'.) After the substantial unity of the passion narratives the diversity of the Gospel accounts of the resurrection appearances is disconcerting. I do not mean just discrepancies in the number of women or angelic figures. In the rigid atmosphere of nineteenth-century England these discrepancies were sufficient to dispel the faith of Ernest Pontifex in *The Way of All Flesh*. Today such differences may still seem odd to the exact scholar in his study but they would occasion no surprise to those acquainted with evidence as given in the police courts.

Much more puzzling is the different overall characters that the accounts have in the different Gospels. In Matthew (28) Jesus appears to the women in Jerusalem and later to his disciples in Galilee. As I have already explained (p. 35) the genuine ending of Mark has probably been lost and in consequence we have no appearance account in the reliable text available to us, though Mark 16.7 seems to point ahead to an appearance to the disciples in Galilee. In Luke (24) Jesus does not appear in person to the women. There are several appearances to the disciples (Peter, the two on the road to Emmaus, the gathered disciples). However it all takes place in the Jerusalem area and apparently all in the course of the first Easter day. This last point contrasts with the same writer's summary at the beginning of Acts (1.1–5) which attributes the appearances to a forty-day period. In John there are appearances to Mary Magdalene and twice, at a week's interval, to the disciples, in Jerusalem (20). Later there is an appearance in Galilee (21, which has some signs of being an appendix to the Gospel – compare 20.30 with 21.24–25). It is also noteworthy that in Luke and John we are presented with a more uncompromisingly material picture than in Matthew. In both the former Gospels Jesus is shown eating common food with his disciples.

Of course, it is not impossible to harmonize the broad

structure of these Gospel accounts but there is clearly a much more fragmented and tangled skein of tradition for the resurrection appearances than for the passion. Nor are the Gospels and Paul's tradition completely four square. It is striking that he omits all reference to the women. It is possible that this is because in the eyes of the male-oriented Jewish law women's testimony would not count as evidence.

I would summarize the burden of the appearance evidence in the following terms. There is a widespread tradition that Jesus showed himself alive to his disciples after his death. During the New Testament period there was a significant number of people alive who would have claimed that they had seen the risen Lord. Nevertheless there was something strange about the experience (the difficulties of recognition which are a feature of each Gospel's account) that gave to the details, if not the primary assertion, a private character which led to the baffling variety of the tradition. In a way the very peculiarity of the testimony makes it seem less likely to be pure invention. If the evangelists composed the accounts out of their heads, why did they give no detailed account of the appearances to Peter (briefly alluded to in Luke 24.34, 1 Cor. 15.5) and to Jesus' half brother James (1 Cor. 15.7)? I believe it is likely to be because these occasions were too intimate for common repetition of their details.

In evaluating this evidence it is important to recognize that the New Testament seems quite able to distinguish between these appearances of the risen Christ which only happened for a limited period, and the sort of visions of Jesus which have been a continuing phenomenon for ecstatically sensitive people in the Church down the ages. The latter (which clearly are no evidence at all for the resurrection – for Catholics they are quite as likely to involve the Virgin Mary as her Son) also occur in the New Testament (for example, Acts 18.9, where the Lord speaks words of comfort to Paul in a dream). However there is no attempt to attach any special significance to them. But is not Paul's Damascus road experience, which he cites in 1 Corinthians 15.8 as part of the resurrection evidence, itself precisely such an ecstatic vision? It might seem so to us, but Paul, who based on it his claim to apostolic authority, is emphatic it is not. Elsewhere (2 Cor. 12.2–4, pretty certainly a coy self-reference) he makes it plain that he has had ecstatic experience, but rather than attempting to build anything on that he deliberately underplays its significance.

A second line of evidence about the resurrection centres on the claim of the empty tomb. The earliest account available to us is in Mark 16.1–8, in which the women going to the tomb on Easter Sunday find the stone rolled away and the sepulchre empty. It is notorious that Paul makes no explicit reference to the empty tomb, though the odd emphasis on the burial in the primitive tradition (1 Cor. 15.4) seems peculiar if it is not pointing implicitly in that direction.

No other topic connected with the resurrection excites such contrasting reactions. A certain school of thought, which tends with unhelpful hyperbole to talk about the resurrection as if it were the best attested fact in all history, regards the empty tomb as providing the crunch argument. Why did the Jewish authorities not nip Christianity in the bud by exhibiting the mouldering body of Jesus to the discomfort and defeat of the disciples? The answer, they suggest, was that it was not to be had; the tomb was empty. Since it is incredible (as indeed it is) that the disciples stole it as an act of deceit, it must be that Jesus rose from the dead. Q.E.D.

The main difficulty about this lies in establishing that Jesus was buried in an identifiable tomb rather than being tossed into a common grave for criminals. Certainly the latter was the frequent Roman custom. Of course, the Gospels tell us that he was buried in just such an identifiable tomb, belonging to Joseph of Arimathea. But might that not be just part of the retrojection of the empty tomb story invented by the piety of the early believers?

There are a number of considerations which tell against that. There is some archaeological evidence to show that not all executed corpses were consigned by the Romans to a common grave, so that the gospel story is not inconceivable. There is the circumstantial evidence of the details given about the roles of Joseph and Nicodemus, neither of whom seem to have played any outstanding part in the life of the early Church, so that the most plausible reason for assigning them an honourable role in Jesus' burial would seem to be that they actually played it. Above all there is the fact that later Jewish anti-Christian polemic always accepts the existence of the tomb and its emptiness and seeks rather to explain it by such implausible devices as theft by the disciples. (The story of the watch in Matthew 27.62–66, 28.11–15 shows that this line of argument must have been used by Jews early on, for here we have an equally implausible Christian story almost certainly made up to counteract it!) If there is force in the common grave argument against the empty tomb it is strange that it did not strike those close in time to the events but had to await the ingenuity of nineteenth-century scholars.

It can also be argued, with some force, that any notion of resurrection would imply an empty tomb for first-century Jews. They held to the strong Hebrew idea of the unitary nature of man. In the often quoted words of H. Wheeler-Robinson, the Hebrews regarded man as 'an animated body not an incarnated soul', an insight which, by the turning of the wheel of intellectual history, we have recaptured after the Cartesian centuries of the ghost in the machine. For such people there could be no idea that Jesus was alive but had left his body behind in the tomb.

The different ways in which the empty tomb tradition is evaluated reflect the way in which theological presupposition and historical evidence interact. The late Professor Geoffrey Lampe, a man of deep Christian conviction and character, believed that Jesus' bones most probably lay in Palestine still because otherwise he would not have shared in the corruption which is part of common human destiny. The argument is a serious one. Against it must be set the consideration, to which I shall return, that Jesus' resurrection was the inauguration of the *ultimate* destiny of all men, so that he rose as 'the first fruits of those who have fallen asleep' (1 Cor. 15.20).

The empty tomb is never presented in the New Testament as a knockdown argument. On the contrary, it needs explanation (the message of the angelic figures in Mark 16.6, Luke 24.4–7; the impetuosity of Peter contrasted with the comprehension of the beloved disciple, John 20.3–9). There has to be a two-way dialogue between history and faith.

If one believes that the tomb was empty, as I do, certain consequences follow. One was succinctly put by Karl Barth* when he said that the empty tomb 'distinguishes the confession that Jesus lives from a mere manner of speaking on the part of believers'. Another thing that the empty tomb says to me is that matter has a destiny, a transformed and transmuted destiny no doubt, but a destiny nevertheless. The material creation is not a transient, even mistaken, episode. Of course that is a deeply mysterious thought (more about it later). The latter part of 1 Corinthians 15 shows Paul grappling with it, not altogether successfully to my mind. One could so easily imagine an apocryphal fragment (from the *Gospel of Geoffrey*, shall we say?) in which the spirit of Christ points the disciples to his abandoned corpse and tells them that he no longer needs it. The canonical writers are wiser than that.

Mention of the apocryphal writings of the second century and later reminds me to point out that in the New Testament there is no account of the resurrection itself, only of its aftermath. Once again the discretion of the evangelists is impressive (though Matthew, always the writer most prone to go for a marvellous tale, gets perilously close in Matthew 28.2–4). The resurrection is unpicturable, though its consequences are not beyond experience. If you can, get hold of a copy of New

Testament Apocrypha and read the purported account of the resurrection in the *Gospel of Peter*. You will see how embarrassingly inadequate was pious fancy to envisage this great act of God.

The circumstantial evidence that I have surveyed is significantly strengthened by some inferential considerations to which we must now turn.

The first is the existence of Sunday as the Christian day of worship. How did it come about that a movement which originated in Judaism, and which for an appreciable time continued in the sabbath worship of the synagogue, came to have as its own special day of the week not the seventh but the first? All the Gospels assert that it was on that day that the tomb was found empty (Mark 16.1 par.) and I think that the most likely explanation for the existence of Sunday as the Lord's day is that from the very first it was known as the day on which Jesus rose from the dead.

The second point, and the most significant of all, is the transformation of the disciples. There can be no reason to doubt that Good Friday saw them demoralized and defeated, fearfully abandoning their master to the fate of crucifixion. The shameful story of their flight and Peter's denial could only have been preserved and repeated because it was part of the record of what actually happened. The pious Jew had an especial horror of crucifixion. Because of a Mosaic curse upon a man hung upon a tree (Deut. 21.23), it appeared to him as a particular sign of divine rejection. We can understand the despair that filled the disciples' hearts when their leader, in whom all their hope for Israel reposed, suffered this ignominious death. A crucified Messiah was an impossibility, the thought a bitter black jest.

A few weeks later the same disciples are proclaiming that Jesus is the Christ, his death part of God's plan. To this they bear steadfast witness in the face of those same authorities who had previously seemed so terrifying. In due course many of them met, with bravery and conviction, deaths as violent as their master's.

It is an astonishing transformation. Something happened to bring it about. Whatever it was it must have been of a magnitude commensurate with the effect it produced. I believe that it was the resurrection of Jesus from the dead.

The final point is one which those outside the Christian faith may well treat with caution and reserve though I believe that it is one which must be taken into account. It is the continuing witness of the Church. I do not mean by that the argument one sometimes hears, that so large and persistent a movement could not have been based on a fallacy. The oddity of human nature is such that that argument is an insecure one. We can all think of movements of considerable stability which have the most peculiar beliefs about their origins. What I do mean is that the Christian testimony to Jesus has always had a special character to it. It has not looked back to Jesus as a venerated founder-figure, in the way that Judaism looks back to Moses or Islam to Muhammad. The authentic note of Christian witness has always been to speak to Jesus as its living Lord, ever contemporary. It is a resurrection faith or it is nothing. For those of us within the community of faith this experience, however fleeting and elusive, is an inescapable part of our understanding of the resurrection.

Something happened. But what? Was it all a psychological phenomenon? In the nineteenth century Ernest Renan said that it was love that brought Jesus back to life. Rudolf Bultmann* – the influential twentieth-century theologian who has displayed a fairly maximal distrust of, and distaste for, history – said that Jesus rose into the faith of his disciples. In this manner of thinking the resurrection is a symbolical (mythical) way of expressing the re-evaluation of Jesus' life and death which his disciples reached after due reflection. Quite frankly, I don't think that begins to be adequate to the phenomena.

Are we to suppose that after the denial and defeat of Calvary it was the taking of a little thought that changed those frightened and disillusioned men into the bold proclaimers of the Lordship of Jesus?

Perhaps, then, it was an abreaction in Peter, after the trauma of the denial, which made him feel that Jesus was alive and this communicated itself, in the fraught atmosphere of that little band, to the other disciples in a sort of psychological chain reaction? But how does that square with the testimony of the appearances scattered in space and time, ending with Paul's Damascus road experience some three years or so after the crucifixion? If it is all in the mind, why do the New Testament writers so persistently present the story as an *event*, strange but actual, leaving its trace in history? Remember that they appear quite capable of identifying ecstatic visionary experiences when they have them.

I believe that the only explanation which is commensurate with the phenomena is that Jesus rose from the dead in such a fashion (whatever that may be) that it is true to say that he is alive today, glorified and exalted but still continuously related in a mysterious but real way with the historical figure who lived and died in first-century Palestine.

Whether you can share that view will depend not only on how you read the evidence but also how the conclusion fits into your view of the world. Does it cohere with the way things are? Is it consonant with the nature of Jesus and the nature of God? (Of course the intellectual traffic flows both ways, but let us concentrate on that direction.)

In the previous two chapters I have discussed Jesus. The view there presented is one that would find its appropriate consummation in the assertion of Paul (probably quoting an earlier formulation) that finally Jesus was 'designated Son of God in power according to the Spirit of holiness by his resurrection from the dead' (Rom. 1.4).

I believe that the resurrection is not only the vindication of Jesus. It is also the beginning of the vindication of God. One of the recurring Old Testament themes in

Israel's turbulent relationship with her God was her reliance upon his *chesed*, his 'steadfast love' as some modern translations finely render it. At the heart of the universe there is One who can be relied upon, whose purposes are purposes of love and will prevail, all signs to the contrary notwithstanding. When Jesus was engaged in controversy with the Sadducees about the ultimate resurrection of all men (Mark 12.18–27 par.) his argument was at root an appeal to this faithfulness of God. He said, 'As for the dead being raised, have you not read in the book of Moses, in the passage about the bush, how God said to him "I am the God of Abraham, the God of Isaac, the God of Jacob"? He is not God of the dead but of the living.' If God is truly Lord, nothing of value can ever be lost in him. That is the only source of human hope. It is the ground of the credibility of the resurrection.

We all have within us the wistful longing that all should be well. Max Horkheimer* characterized it as the desire that 'the murderer should not triumph over his innocent victim'. In the cross of Christ we see innocence nailed to the tree. In the resurrection we see God's assertion – and so his own vindication – that this is not the final word on the human condition.

If death was not the final word for Jesus it is also the Christian conviction that it is not the final word for us either. 'As in Adam all die, even so in Christ shall all be made alive' (1 Cor. 15.22). It is part of the grand picture of salvation that his destiny is to be ours also.

The certain fact of mortality is one that places a large question mark over human life. It is a commonplace that death has replaced sex as the great taboo of contemporary Western culture. We conspire to put it out of sight. Not for us the *memento mori*. But out of sight is certainly not out of mind.

Our attitude to death is compounded of two conflicting insights. One acknowledges the reality of death; the disintegration of the body is a genuine end. But within us there is a second insight which rebels against that

conclusion. We have a tenacious longing to escape annihil-
ation, an instinctive aspiration to survival. Where personal hope has been abandoned this longing for continuity
is transferred to some communal entity. The Race or the
Party will be perpetuated. However, even if the contin-
uance of these abstractions met our needs (which it does
not) it would provide no qualitative solution but simply
a quantitative lengthening of the time-scale over which
the problem makes itself felt. As we saw in Chapter 2, the
long-term prospects for our environment, or even for the
universe as a whole, are pretty black. Ahead lie the sun's
explosion and the decay or collapse of the whole world.

Christian understanding takes both these insights about
death seriously. It does not deny the reality of death –
Gethsemane makes that point – but it does deny that it is
the ultimate reality. The final word is always God's. We
do not proclaim a message of survival but a gospel of
death (real death) and resurrection (God's real re-creative
act of a whole man, not a disembodied spirit).

A destiny beyond death is central to the problem of
theodicy,* that critical theological question of the vindication of God in the face of the terrors and suffering of
his creation. Many contemporary Christians seem reluctant to acknowledge this. The taunt about 'pie in the sky
when you die' has bitten deep. Of course, the hope of a
future life is no reason for neglecting the pursuit of love
and justice in this one. Of course, the hope of a future life
freed from the pains and limitations of this one does not
one whit remove the agony of those limitations and pains.
The death of a child from leukaemia is not explained
away by the belief that the child has a destiny and
happiness beyond the grave. To suppose the contrary
would indeed be 'pie in the sky'. But without some future
hope, the bitterness of this present world would be bitter
indeed. What then would we make of those who die with
their lives manifestly unfulfilled or grievously distorted
or diminished by cruel circumstance? Or what would we
make of those gains of character wrought by painful
moral struggle? Are they merely transient epiphenomena

91

on the stage of the world? In the end are we all just broken pots cast on to the universal rubbish heap? Or can it be that the potter is at work moulding us in a process which here finds no final achievement and so must continue in another life hereafter?

Because Christianity takes from Judaism the realistic recognition that man is an animated body and not an incarnated soul, it looks, not for the survival of some tenuous spiritual part of him, but for the resurrection of a transformed whole man. Is such a belief credible?

At the start of the discussion it is good to acknowledge our limited powers of a priori anticipation of what can prove to be the case. The history of science is full of the discovery of phenomena previously inconceivable or even asserted to be downright impossible. At the turn of the century Lord Kelvin* was able to assure the biologists that the earth could only be twenty million years old. He had calculated how long the sun could shine, deriving its energy from gravitational contraction, and that was how the sum worked out. Of course, so short a time-scale was inadequate to accommodate the fossil record of evolution as the biologists interpreted it. I believe that one palaeontologist had the temerity to ask the grand old man of physical science whether there could be some unknown source of energy which would have kept the sun shining for substantially longer. Kelvin told him that it could not be so. (We know now that the sun derives its energy principally from nuclear reactions like the carbon cycle.*)

As with the resurrection of Jesus, so with the idea of a general human resurrection, there have been attempts to express the hope in as maximally symbolic and as minimally objective a way as possible. After death God will continue to remember me or the good which was in my life. I find such attempts wholly inadequate to a coherent understanding of how things are. The hope of resurrection is very different from being a fly stuck in the amber of divine thought. The latter is a static picture which confuses biography with personality. The former is dynamic and meets the need for process and fulfilment which we have identified in the human condition.

We know that there is nothing significant about the material which at any one time constitutes our body. After about seven years almost all the atoms have been changed. It is the pattern they form which persists and evolves. We are liberated, therefore, from the quaint medieval picture of the reassembly of a body from its scattered components. In very general terms it is not difficult to imagine that pattern recreated (the body resurrected) in some other world. If you like, the mathematical apparatus of projection from one space to another provides a logical basis for such a thought. In this way we perceive the possibility of continuity without material identity.

Of course there are a great many puzzles of detail about this blithe suggestion. If the laws of 'matter' in the new world are the same as those in this will they not reproduce its physical ills? If they are vastly different, will that not tend to destroy continuity? At what moment, so to speak, is the projection made? If at the moment of death it will recreate a corpse. If at some earlier moment, is not then all the subsequent earthly experience beyond that point made irrelevant?

One might begin to grope at speculative notions which might provide some shadowy clues to surmounting these difficulties. I think that that activity would almost certainly be a waste of time, because we do not have enough knowledge on which to ground it. One learns pretty soon in science that there are times when problems are ripe for solution and times when they are not. The history of our evolving understanding of the structure of matter has been one of the unravelling of successive layers – atoms, nuclei, 'elementary' particles, quarks and gluons. At each stage in that process people who prematurely tried to guess what the next level would be before it began to become accessible to experiment were invariably wide of the mark. They were like generals fighting the battles of the last war. So it is with the resurrection. We do not have enough to go on for detailed theory making. But we do have the resurrection of Jesus to tell us that these things can be.

The idea that God's purposes find their fulfilment through process and that process continues beyond the grave, removes from the life to come that air of heavenly boredom often so vividly expressed in the pages of the hymnbook ('and gaze and gaze on thee'). Beyond that there is little that we can say. In the end even Dante's imagination faltered:

> High phantasy lost power and here broke off;
> Yet, as a wheel moves swiftly, free from jars,
> My will and my desire were turned by love,
>
> The love that moves the sun and the other stars.

NINE

The Sequel

Alfred Loisy* remarked that Jesus foretold the coming of the Kingdom but it was the Church which came. If you search today for the nearest contemporary equivalent to the scene at the Last Supper – always excluding those vital and mysterious words 'This is my body', 'This is my blood' – you will find it in a pious Jewish home on a Friday evening rather than at Papal High Mass in St Peter's on a Sunday. The Trinitarian dogmas of the Councils of Nicea (AD 325) and Constantinople (AD 381) and the christological dogmas of the Council of Chalcedon (AD 451), with their Hellenistic philosophical talk of person (*hypostasis*) and substance (*ousia*), speak a very different language from that of the New Testament. Even within the New Testament it is obvious that, on the one hand the band of disciples following Jesus in the days of his earthly ministry, and on the other the post-Easter Church, are strikingly different. How could it be otherwise? With the experience of the cross and resurrection behind them the members of the early Church knew more.

No one could deny that there has been considerable development in the thought and practice of Christianity over the centuries which separate us from the events in which it took its origin. The question is whether that process represents the fruition or the distortion and destruction of what was there from the beginning. In broad outline, I would claim that the development has been towards making explicit what was implicit, rather than creating something other, along with an inescapable response to changing social circumstances. As far as the latter is concerned, it is inevitable that a sect driven partly underground by persecution, and a religion recognized and encouraged by the state, are going to have different forms of organization and activity, and demand different degrees of commitment from the generality of their adherents. Many Christians have seen in the embrace of Constantine the kiss of death. There is no doubt that state approval was an ambiguous blessing, but the Church found within itself its own immuno-suppressive system, for example in the development of monasticism as an antidote to the infection of worldly power. The Church has had many failures (I shall return to that) but it has also from within, time and time again, come upon the judgement of the Kingdom, the sovereign rule of God.

We are concerned at present primarily with the Christian world view. As dogma developed, has it so obscured the original insights that the picture has been changed beyond recognition? I think not. Let us consider the development of one dogma, at once both fundamental to Christianity and strange to common sense, the doctrine of the Trinity, Three Persons and One God.

The typical New Testament view is enshrined in the Pauline phrase 'God our Father and the Lord Jesus Christ' (see p. 62). It is pretty clear that this cannot represent an intellectually stable position. It is, rather, an interim statement, an immediate response to the phenomenon of the Lordship of Jesus combined in uneasy juxtaposition with Jewish recognition of the one true God. In what sense can Jesus be Lord when God himself is quintessentially the Lord? Paul's statement is what a physicist would call 'phenomenological'. In the dialogue between experiment and theory there are these useful middlemen, the phenomenologists, who try to encapsulate experimental data in suggestive formulae, without being able to give a fundamental explanation for the form chosen. The pursuit of that deeper comprehension is the task of the theoretical physicist, and till he has been successful a full understanding has not been gained.

The pursuit of that deeper understanding of the Pauline

phenomenology was what set Christianity off on the path that led in the end to Trinitarian doctrine. I have already tried in the preceding chapters to explain why Christians were driven to find in the man Jesus elements also of the divine. But this could not mean that he exhausted the godhead. The heavens were not empty during his earthly life; indeed he constantly prayed to God his Father. There is therefore both an identity and a distinction in Jesus' relation with the divine Father. It is the preservation of that distinction which drove New Testament writers, whilst attributing to Jesus an authority which goes beyond the human, to be extremely wary of calling him God.

More slowly still, the Church became aware of the presence of God in yet another way. It felt in its midst the power of God which it referred to as his Spirit. In Old Testament times men had often spoken of the spirit of the Lord. (The Hebrew word *ruach* also means breath and wind, as does the Greek *pneuma*.) It came upon the prophets as the source of their inspiration. It had been brooding on the chaos of the deep in creation (Gen. 1.2). The Church felt the activity of the Spirit with such intensity that it no longer seemed appropriate to speak of it as if it were just an emanation of power from God but rather it seemed necessary to recognize it as the presence of God himself. The spirit had become the Spirit, so to speak. Yet the characteristic activity of the Spirit was to move the believer to pray to God (Rom. 8.14–16, 26–27). Once again there was an element of distinctness to be preserved.

The Spirit was (and is) the most elusive element in the experience of God. The New Testament is often very confused about him. In a single verse of his letter to the Romans (8.9) Paul can speak of 'the Spirit', 'the Spirit of God' and 'the Spirit of Christ'. The much more characteristic New Testament phrase is the binitarian 'God our Father and the Lord Jesus Christ' rather than the trinitarian 'the grace of our Lord Jesus Christ, the love of God and the fellowship of the Holy Spirit' (2 Cor. 13.14). It took several centuries for a recognition of the Spirit's divinity and distinctiveness to gain universal acceptance in the Church. Nevertheless, in the end there did not appear to be a stable position, adequate to experience, which did not take account of this fact.

I think it is important to recognize that the doctrine of the Trinity arose in this way, as a response to phenomena rather than an ungrounded metaphysical speculation. It is a summary of experience rather than a puzzling piece of divine arithmetic. We know God as Creator and Ruler; in pictorial terms, as God above us. (Spatial metaphors seem unavoidable, and are certainly not circumvented by the modern fashion of replacing height by depth.) We know God in Jesus, having lived a human life but declared Lord by the resurrection: God alongside us, as you might say. We know God at work within us, in the depth of our own being. All these experiences are distinct, but they are manifestations of the one true God. There seems to be an inescapable threeness within the Unity. I believe, therefore, that the doctrine of the Trinity is not so much an attempt to construct a metaphysic of the divine nature as to do justice to the richness and complexity of the divine revelation.

This phenomenological approach to the Trinity (the economic Trinity, as the theologians call it) liberates us from the hectoring and self-confident tone of such statements as the *Quicunque Vult* (the so-called Athanasian creed – nothing to do with Athanasius!) This creed drones on with the utmost assurance about the ineffable details of the divine nature ('This is the Catholic Faith which except a man believe faithfully he cannot be saved . . .'). What Trinitarian theology in fact provides for us is not a blueprint of the godhead but an epitome of what he has been pleased to reveal to us of his nature.

It is often a mark of a good theory in science that it yields unexpected understanding, going beyond the compass of the data it was invented to explain. This is, of course, a very exciting and convincing thing when it happens. Paul Dirac invented a celebrated equation to describe the behaviour of the electron. His motivation was to satisfy simultaneously the requirements of quantum mechanics and special relativity. The Dirac equation achieves this non-trivial synthesis in an elegant and satisfying manner. It was a substantial additional bonus over and above that when Dirac realized that his equation also afforded the explanation of a fact which up till then had proved inexplicable, namely that the magnetic properties of the electron are twice as intense as one would naively have expected.

The doctrine of the Trinity has this bonus character of affording something extra. By pointing to a trinity within the godhead it offers us an insight into that continuous exchange of love between the Persons which makes sense of the fundamental Christian assertion that God is love. Love is not a passive disposition but an active relation. In tonic contrast to the static perfection of the God of the philosophers, Trinitarianism has a dynamic quality about it. This relational Trinitarianism was the basis of Augustine's famous analogy of the trinity of love:

$$\text{lover} \quad \text{beloved} : \text{Father} \quad \text{Son}$$
$$\underset{\text{love}}{\underleftrightarrow{\qquad\qquad}} \quad \underset{\text{Spirit}}{\underleftrightarrow{\qquad\qquad}}$$

In drawing such a diagram am I not beginning the process for which I reproved the unknown author of the *Quicunque Vult*, namely the attempt to explain the details of the divine nature? Was there ever since Babel a more overweeningly ambitious project? The more discerning writers on the Trinity have always been aware of the danger.

Augustine prefaced his great work on the Trinity with the disarming words:

> I ask my readers to make common cause with me when they share my convictions; to keep an open mind when they share my doubts. I ask them to correct me if I make a mistake but to return to my way of thinking if they do.

Later in the same work he wrote:

> When the question is asked 'Three whats?' human language labours altogether under great poverty of speech. The answer is given 'Three persons', not that it might be spoken but that it might not be left unspoken.

We have already had cause to note (p. 68) the limitations under which theology inevitably labours.

Since Genesis asserts that man was made in the image of God (Gen. 1.26) Augustine believed that it would be in human nature that the best clues would be found to such a degree of understanding of the divine nature as it is possible for men to achieve. We may well feel that he chose the right place to look. All our most significant experience is that which exercises us most profoundly as persons. Augustine had deeply intuitive powers of introspection which enabled him in many ways to anticipate the sorts of insight later afforded by depth psychology. Within the human *mens* (more than mind, rather our psyche) he detected *memoria* (deeper than memory, our unconscious mind, the fount of all conscious thought and so analogous to the Father, who is the fount of being), *intelligentia* (understanding, the articulate expressive part of personality and so analogous to the Son in whom God manifests himself) and *voluntas* (will, the spring of action, which for Augustine was love, and analogous to the Spirit). It is an analysis of great subtlety and penetration. Modern psychology, despite its conflicting detailed pictures, is agreed in seeing in man not just a self-conscious ego but a complex personality with more than one pole to the interior life (be it Jung's ego and self or Freud's ego, super-ego and id). Is it then surprising that the divine life should exhibit a Trinitarian complexity? Trinitarian doctrine is not just a papering over of the cracks of an underlying tritheism. It has the right 'feel' about it as an insight into the nature of the Creator of men.

Those who believe that the Spirit of God is at work in the world must expect that divine revelation, however highly focused it was in the life and death and resurrection of Jesus, is not solely confined to the period and place of the incarnation. That does not mean that the other loci of revelation are easy to identify. They are not contained in an infallible book, or an infallible Church, or an infallible authority within that Church. Nevertheless the Spirit's work is a continuing one.

For the Christian that insight affords an explanation of the puzzle presented by the fourth Gospel. I have already said (p. 46) that this remarkable book contains both significant historical tradition and also majestic discourses which compel attention and raise hope but which may not actually be words of Jesus uttered during his earthly life. Their authority can be seen as deriving from the work of the Spirit guiding the reflections of a follower of Jesus as he pondered deeply on the significance of his master's earthly life. Within a Trinitarian understanding we can receive them as the words of the risen Lord.

In a similar way, for the believer those parts of the synoptics which we believe to be the creation of the early Church nevertheless have an authority, though they cannot be used for the sort of evidential considerations which have been our main concern in this book.

This is all very well, you may say, but you are avoiding the main issue raised by a chapter heading reading 'The Sequel'. You argued that in Jesus we see God's self-manifestation. His life and death and resurrection are the irrupting into the world of a new regime, the Kingdom of God. If that were really so would not the sequel demonstrate it more convincingly? It would be hard to maintain that history AD has had a different and better character than history BC. What difference has it all made, and if none, does that not cast doubt on the claims being made? Above all; look at the Church, divided by internecine quarrels, often in collusion with dubious political authority, frequently intolerantly persecuting those without the confines of its orthodoxy.

No one can deny that here is a serious argument. Any Christian must feel deep penitence and shame at the thought of the Crusades, the Inquisition, the blasphemy of the wars of religion. The record of Christian colonial powers in contact with 'primitive' people is not always one of which we can feel proud.

However the account is not all written on the debit side of the ledger. In the pioneering of hospitals and education, in the improvement in the status of women (whatever blind spots still remain), the Church has a record in which the Christian can take some comfort. To an extent that we seldom appreciate, we people in the West are living on inherited moral capital which is being consumed as the Christian fabric of society diminishes. We begin to feel the loss when we contemplate some of the ruthless individualism of the present age. We are losing that sense of the common good which certainly owed a great deal to Christianity.

Secondly, as we noted earlier, the Church has shown some capacity, analogous to that of a healthy body, to heal its own sores and wounds. When the abuse of the sale of indulgences spreads there arises a Luther to denounce it and proclaim the free grace of God. In our own day the liberation theologians of South America put in question our bourgeois establishment acquiescence in things as they are.

At root the problem is, Why does not God make his presence more visible in the world, his power more manifest? The work of his grace in remedying the flaws of sinful humanity seems so slow and so partial. Even in the lives of the saints we see the same problem – Francis, the book denier; Augustine, in the grip of predestinarian logic.

I do not know the answer to this mystery. It seems that it is God's way to work slowly and almost secretly. When we think of all those thousands of millions of years which elapsed from the big bang till the universe saw the emergence of life, we see that he is not a God in a hurry. He is a God of process and not of magic. Perhaps there is no other way for love to work if it is to respect the integrity of the beloved.

TEN

Other Views of the World

I have tried, as far as I am able, to present the Christian view of the world and the reason why I accept it. But all the time I am conscious that we live in a world with many competing views expressed about it. I have to attempt to say what I make of that. Those other views cannot just be swept under the mental carpet.

The problem occurs at two levels. One is represented by my non-religious humanist friends. They include people for whose integrity I have the highest regard. What is at issue between us is the existence of a religious dimension to life, an experience of the Other, together with the credibility of a purpose in the world and a destiny for man beyond the commonly acknowledged circumstances of the way of the world. As far as religious experience is concerned, I cannot deny my own and I can only regret that my humanist friends do not share it or do not recognize it when they do. As far as purpose and destiny are concerned, we are reading the same facts in different ways and I have already spent much space trying to indicate why I see things the way I do. Because a religious view is always a discernment of a further level in life it is difficult to express the difference between myself and my humanist friends without using a metaphor which seems smugly congratulatory to the religious. I hope my friends will forgive me if I say that we seem like people viewing a terrain, some of whom say it is a two-dimensional backdrop and others that it is a three-dimensional landscape.

Much more worrying is the problem posed by the adherents of other faiths. We have so much in common,

Broadly speaking, we agree that there is a religious dimension to life, a purpose in the world, a destiny for men. It is agreed between us that the terrain under survey is a three-dimensional landscape. However when we come to say in detail what is in it our descriptions do not tally. When one man says that he sees a mountain where another man maintains that he sees a lake, it is not surprising if an independent bystander is liable to conclude that both are retailing their dreams rather than giving an account of how things are.

The difficulty is intensified by a simple sociological reflection. It would be disingenuous to maintain that my being a Christian is totally unconnected with the fact that I was born in Britain. Had I been born in India the chances are that I would be a Hindu. Had I been born in Saudi Arabia it would have been a virtual certainty that I would have been a Muslim. Does that mean that once again religion is threatening to dissolve into a sea of culturally determined conflicting opinions?

The entry of cultural factors into one's understanding of the world does not imply the exit of truth from it. After all, modern science has grown up in the same Western cultural milieu which is also the sociological setting of my Christianity. With science's ability to appeal to public impersonal knowledge it has been able to spread from its cultural place of origin more successfully than Christianity, though it is probably true even today that the accident of my birthplace increased my chances of having a productive career as a scientist as well as my chances of being a Christian.

There are two things that I want to say about the puzzle of the diversity of the world religions. The first is that I do not doubt that true experience of God is to be found within them. Of course, one traditional Christian attitude was to see them only as the loci of error and blindness. I feel sure that this is wrong. It implies the extraordinary conclusion that God has left himself without witness in the world at most times and in most places. If the Word is the light that enlightens every man, that would be an intolerable conclusion to reach. It is also contrary to our observation. Across the cultural gaps and the differences that divide us, we can discern in some adherents of other faiths a holiness and depth of experience which commands our silent respect and recognition. I have already quoted William James (p. 31) on the common character of the mystical experience.

Having gladly paid tribute to the authenticity of religious experience outside the acknowledged confines of Christianity, I want to go on to say as my second point that it would be a grave mistake to suppose that there are no significant differences between the world's religions. Their views of the world certainly differ. For example, it seems to me that the religions originating in the Near East (Judaism, Christianity, Islam) have a more realistic view of the world and the evil in it than do the religions of the Far East. I cannot accept that the suffering of the world is an illusion from which release is to be sought by enlightenment. Rather, the cross of Christ demonstrates the objective and inescapable character of that suffering. A Buddhist might find a crucifix an ugly and degrading symbol of suffering. I believe that on the cross Jesus opened his arms to embrace the bitterness of the world.

Above all there is the fundamental difference between Christianity and other religions about the significance of Jesus. There has been a good deal of very sensitive appreciation of the human figure of Jesus by men of all religions but, of course, it falls short of the Christian claim that in him 'God was reconciling the world to himself' (2 Cor. 5.19). Gandhi, for instance, drew considerable inspiration from the New Testament. However he said that for him the question of whether Jesus actually existed or not did not matter, for in either case we would still have the Sermon on the Mount. But the Christian gospel is not primarily concerned with good advice but with salvation, an act of power by God to redeem the marred character of humanity. It centres on the God-man Jesus as the unique meeting of God's love and man's need. If he did not exist Christianity collapses.

If the Christian estimate of Jesus is true, as I believe it is, then at bottom all human experience of God flows through the unique junction of the incarnate Word and ultimately all human hope takes its origin in Jesus Christ. To say that is not to deny that other religions may have important insights of which Christianity stands in need for its completion. It is part of what theologians call the 'scandal of particularity' that if God became man he had to do so at a particular time and a particular place. The limitations thereby accepted doubtless meant that not all that could be known by men was fully articulated in that particular cultural setting. We have already considered in Chapter 9 the sequel within Christianity itself and argued that the Spirit continued at work to interpret the significance of Jesus' life. (We must carefully distinguish between the once-for-all event of Jesus and the understanding of it whose unravelling is a continuing process.) I would not wish to deny the activity of the same Spirit outside the visible confines of the Church. That carries with it the implication of things to be learnt from the non-Christian faiths (and, I believe, in the questions that they put, from those of no faith at all). However, because I believe that the Word became flesh in Jesus, I believe that he is God's ultimate channel of self-communication with all men. More know him than know him by name.

I realize that the notion of that last sentence, which thinks of the people of other religions as, so to speak, anonymous Christians, is one that they may find offensive. It smacks of religious imperialism, a Christian take-over bid. Yet it has a long history in the Church, which in the first centuries had suffcient insight not to write off people like Socrates and Plato as benighted pagans and so accorded them a sort of honorary Christian status. I would want to purge the 'anonymous Christian' idea of all triumphalist overtones of annexation, but in the end it is the only concept which does justice both to the authentic experience of God manifested in other religions and also to my conviction that in Jesus God was revealed in a unique way.

But if Christianity is really true, why are there these diverse religions flourishing in the world? Why do I have to appeal to this strangely anonymous presence of Christ? I do not know the answer to these questions. It is part of the mystery of the hidden character of God. It may be that, out of a delicate respect for our independent integrity, he does not overwhelm us by his unequivocal presence. He is always the elusive veiled One beyond our immediate apprehension. That is the way the world is. God does not shrivel us by the bright beam of his glory but he allows his light to diffuse and be refracted by the myriad cultural prisms of men.

ELEVEN

The Christian View of the World

It is time to try to pull some threads together, to epitomize the Christian view. A convenient organizing principle can, perhaps, be provided by the idea of the *logos*, the Word or articulate declaration of God, his means of self-manifestion.

Everyone knows that John's Gospel begins with a prologue about the Word:

> In the beginning was the Word and the Word was with God and the Word was God. He was in the beginning with God. All things were made through him and without him was not anything made that was made. In him was life and the life was the light of men.
>
> (John 1.1–4)

Behind the intelligibility of the universe, its openness to the investigation of science, there lies, I believe, the fact of the Word of God. The Word is God's agent in creation, impressing his rationality on the world. That same Word is also the light of men, giving us thereby access to the rationality that is in the world. If science is the pale reflection of the rationality which is in God, so our experience of beauty is a pale reflection of his joy, our moral insights the pale reflection of his purposes of love. Nor, I believe, is it mistaken to see that same Word at work, under different cultural constraints, in the religious experience of all mankind.

Thus far the Christian may have many fellow-travellers in his company. Augustine, in Book VII of the *Confessions*, records that he found similar thoughts in the writings of the neoplatonists. What he did not find written there, and what constitutes the parting of the ways for the Christian from many of his friends, is the assertion that 'the Word became flesh and dwelt among us, full of grace and truth' (John 1.14). God acted to make himself known in the way most directly intelligible to men, not in the generalities of world structure but in the particularity of a human life and a human death *sub Pontio Pilato*. The eternal was subject to the contingency of history, the absolute caught in the cultural cage of time and place.

Ancient civilizations had their tales of the gods come among men. Part of the attraction of modern science fiction, with its talk of other worlds and other beings, is that it ministers to the sublimated desire we have to be in touch with someone from outside the confined world of men. The talking animals of children's stories are another aspect of the same desire. There is a deep feeling within man that he is not complete without Another and there is a deep longing for that Other to make himself known. We are thirsty for God. He is to be found, not in the shadowy figures of mythology nor in the imaginative creations of men, but in the concrete historical figure of Jesus of Nazareth.

Such an astonishing assertion cannot be lightly assented to. It requires an assessment of the events to see if there is a glimmer of possibility that they might bear that weight of interpretation. Jesus came teaching with special authority ('Amen, I say to you . . .') and in a special relationship of intimacy with God ('Abba'). Those who knew him, monotheistic Jews though they were, could without a sense of absurdity or blasphemy call him Lord, the accepted circumlocution for the divine name, and could speak of God our Father and the Lord Jesus Christ in the same breath. Yet he died the shameful death of crucifixion, deserted by men and apparently abandoned by God. Something happened to change the débâcle of Good Friday into the confidence of Pentecost. The earliest traditions assert that it was the raising of Jesus from death by God on Easter Day. Paul could appeal to the testimony of living witnesses to the fact. The story of Jesus seems to me to be commensurate with the Christian claims about him.

These claims are further strengthened by the insight they afford into the deepest mystery of the way the world is, the prevalence of pain and suffering. Christianity cannot explain the origin of the marredness which we see around us but it points to God's deepest involvement and identity in these contradictions of the world. Both the pain and the hope that are in the world need to find their place in its understanding. They meet in the cross and resurrection of Jesus.

To me this Christian world view has the mark of truth, a coherence, a degree of realism and an adequate complexity, which match the strange way the world is.

TWELVE

Envoi

I hope that this book has had the tone of a coolly rational discourse. We have considered the evidence. I have tried to show that Christianity offers a coherent picture of the way the world is which matches the complexity and strangeness that we find in it. As I acknowledged at the beginning, I have not been able to *prove* Christianity for you any more than you could demonstrate to me beyond a peradventure whatever view of the world you hold. When you come to think about it, there is very little of interest that is susceptible to that sort of proof. Pythagoras' Theorem, no doubt, within the axioms of Euclidean geometry. Just try to defeat in argument the solipsist who maintains that you and I are figments of his imagination. He's wrong, of course, but it's not possible to demonstrate it in the way that one can establish a proposition in mathematics.

The discussion that a book like this presents is addressed to the mind. Our rational faculties are very important and their exercise can save us from all sorts of folly. However we are a great deal more than minds and a real view of the world will have to engage our whole personalities. That is why religions always speak of an act of faith, a response at the deepest levels of our being to that One who is the ground of our being. In the end a religious view of the world is not a philosophical attitude but a personal commitment. Some form of leap of faith is inevitable. I do not think that it is a question of shutting our eyes and hoping for the best in a blind lunge at reality. Of course we should look before we leap. Faith cannot be proved, but it is not unmotivated. If this book can help some to perceive something of the motivation of a Christian understanding of the world I shall be well content. But do not overestimate what has been achieved thereby. It is not the end but the beginning.

Appendix

This is a very personal selection of books which I have found enjoyable and which carry a little further some of the topics discussed.

Top of the list is the Bible. The New Testament is essential reading for anyone with a serious concern for Christianity. Since its writers were soaked in the Jewish scriptures one also needs an acquaintance with the Old Testament, in itself very worth while because of the vitality and fruitfulness of Israel's religion. It may seem a bit of a tall order to get to grips with all this from near scratch. I would suggest reading the Gospels of Mark and John first, then some of the Pauline epistles. The latter are made more accessible if one uses what is effectively an interpretative paraphrase:

J. B. Phillips: *Letters to Young Churches* (Fontana 1971). Some form of New Testament Commentary is essential. I would suggest:

A. E. Harvey: *Companion to the New Testament* (Oxford/Cambridge University Presses 1979). An excellent account of the life of Jesus, written in old age by the foremost British New Testament scholar of his day, is:

C. H. Dodd: *The Founder of Christianity* (Fontana 1973), very strongly recommended. For more detail on critical questions try:

J. A. T. Robinson: *Can We Trust the New Testament?* (Mowbray 1977), which also contains an account of its author's rather idiosyncratic ideas about the early dating of the New Testament documents. A detailed and scholarly discussion of the central question of the resurrection is given by:

G. O'Collins: *The Easter Jesus* (Darton, Longman and Todd 1980).

Some of the signals of Transcendence that the world displays are discussed with attractive perceptiveness by:

P. L. Berger: *A Rumour of Angels* (Penguin 1970).
This book is the more remarkable because Berger is a sociologist whose professional writings have been critical of religion. Anyone who wants to see set out a systematic account of Christian belief could not do better than read:

J. Burnaby: *The Belief of Christendom* (SPCK 1975).
To see how such belief impinges on life read:

H. A. Williams: *The True Wilderness* (Fontana 1976).

If anyone wants to follow up some of the science possible sources are:

J. Monod: *Chance and Necessity* (Fontana 1974);
J. C. Polkinghorne: *The Particle Play* (W. H. Freeman 1979);
S. Weinberg: *The First Three Minutes* (Fontana 1978).
The ideas of Prigogine referred to in Chapter 3 are surveyed in:

I. Prigogine: *From Being to Becoming* (W. H. Freeman 1979), a book ostensibly for the general reader but in fact technically quite difficult.

Glossary

In the text mention is made of both persons and ideas drawn from the worlds of science and theology. Not all these references will be familiar to every reader. This glossary provides some brief background notes.

Apocryphal gospels Writings, principally of the second century AD, which may preserve some fragments of historical tradition but which contain many legendary stories concocted to please pious imagination. Several of these gospels are impregnated with the gnostic heresy, that is, they see Christ as the figure of a spiritual redeemer delivering the enlightened from the trap of the flesh.

Apophatic theology The tradition which emphasizes the mystery, otherness and unknowability of God. It has been stronger in the contemplative Eastern Orthodox Church than in the rationally-minded Latin Church of the West. A favourite image is of Moses entering the cloud and darkness of Sinai to meet the Lord (Exod. 19).

Aramaic The Semitic language spoken by Jesus and his contemporaries. It originated in Syria (Aram) and spread throughout the Near East, replacing Hebrew as the common tongue of Palestine.

Archetypes Powerful symbols which, according to Jung (q.v.) and his followers, are active in the collective unconscious as centres of psychic energy.

Arrow of time If one takes a film of an elementary dynamical process (the collision of two point-like particles, say) then the film makes sense whether it is run forwards or backwards. In other words, there is no natural direction of time for such systems. On the other hand, if one takes a complicated dynamical system (the bouncing of a rubber ball, say), the film run backwards does not make sense (because the bounces get higher and higher instead of diminishing). Thus complicated dynamical systems do possess a natural direction of 'time's arrow'. It turns out to correspond to the direction of increasing entropy (q.v.).

Augustine One of the greatest thinkers in the history of the Church. He flourished in the later fourth and early fifth centuries and was the dominating influence in Western theology for a thousand years. His *Confessions* tell the story of his spiritual pilgrimage which only brought him to orthodox Christian faith in middle life. Profound as his understanding was, his thought was not free from flaws, particularly in his views on the transmission of original sin, the nature of sexuality, and the predestinating irresistibility of God's grace.

Bardeen, J., Cooper, L.N., Schrieffer, J.R. A triumvirate, usually abbreviated to BCS, who successfully explained the phenomenon of superconductivity (q.v.) They were deservedly awarded the Nobel Prize in 1972. John Bardeen is the only man to have shared in two Nobel Prizes for Physics.

Barth, K. One of the dominant figures of twentieth-century theology. His approach (called dialectical or crisis theology) places great emphasis on the word of God and proclaims a divorce between revelation and reason (to a far too absolute degree, in my opinion). Barth, though Swiss, played a leading role in the opposition of the confessing church in Germany to Nazism.

Big bang The galaxies are observed to be all receding from each other (the expansion of the universe). Therefore extrapolation into the past makes them draw closer and closer together until they reach that singular state of collapsed matter where everything has contracted to a point. It appears that the present universe originated from this singularity some fifteen thousand million years ago. The resulting explosive expansion of matter is called the big bang.

Bultmann, R. A dominant figure in twentieth-century New Testament theology. His programme of demythologizing sought to rid Christianity of the embarrassments of a first-century world view and to re-interpret the gospel in existentialist terms. It is now widely recognized that Bultmann was far less successful in separating baby and bathwater than he had supposed and that his theology was unduly anthropocentric.

Carbon cycle The nuclear fusion process, first suggested by Hans Bethe, in which four protons combine to form a helium nucleus. The resulting loss of mass is liberated as energy (according to $E = mc^2$) and provides an energy source for stars like the sun.

Christology That part of theology which has as its aim the understanding of the person and work of Jesus Christ. The classical problem of Christology is to reconcile the humanity and divinity which orthodox Christian understanding ascribes to Jesus. The celebrated definition of the Council of Chalcedon in AD 451 is more a marking out of the area of orthodox discourse (inevitably in the philosophical language of the time) than a resolution of the paradox.

Dark companion of Sirius A heavy 'dead' star which is a partner of Sirius. It has exhausted its energy and so does not shine but its presence is known by its gravitational effects on the Dog Star.

Dirac, P.A.M. The greatest British theoretical physicist of this century. His achievements include the quantum mechanical equation which describes the behaviour of an electron in a mannner consistent with the requirements of special relativity, and the invention of quantum field theory (q.v.).

Einstein–Podolsky–Rosen paradox A consequence of quantum theory, first pointed out by Einstein and two young associates in 1934, by which two particles which have once interacted continue in certain ways to be able to influence each other even if they have subsequently become widely separated. This counter-intuitive 'togetherness in separation' struck Einstein as so strange that he thought it must show that quantum theory is in some way incomplete. The more general view is simply that it reveals a surprising non-locality in the theory. The correctness of the effect has recently received experimental confirmation.

Entropy An important quantity in thermodynamics (q.v.). It measures the degree of disorder in a system and for isolated (closed) systems entropy increases with time (the second law of thermodynamics). A glass may shatter into pieces but the fragments will not spontaneously coalesce to form a glass; that is, the movement is in the direction of increasing disorder. Living things are open systems (that is, they are not closed but interact with their environment). This enables them to succeed in producing their own order at the expense of exporting disorder (entropy) into the environment.

Eschatology The theology of the last things. In particular it is concerned with the idea that this present age will come to a final end and God's power and righteousness, presently hidden, will be manifestly vindicated in a new age. Christian thought sees in the present activity of the Kingdom of God (q.v.) an anticipation of that ultimate vindication. This is the notion of realized eschatology, that the present is a mixture of the old and new ages.

Feuerbach, L. A thinker of the early nineteenth century who thought that all statements about God are really projected statements about man. Thus, in his view, theology gives way to anthropology. Feuerbach greatly influenced many people, including Karl Marx.

Formalism The rigorous expression of a scientific theory, usually in mathematical form.

Form criticism The study of the individual stories and sayings which make up the Gospels and which are believed to have circulated independently in oral tradition before being collected and written down.

Fourth Gospel A coy way of referring to the gospel of John, which recognizes its startling differences from the three synoptic Gospels (q.v.).

General relativity The modern theory of gravity invented by Einstein in 1916. It represents gravitational effects as being due to the curvature of space-time. The beauty of this idea of replacing mechanics by geometry, and the elegant economy of the mathematical formulation of the theory, have long commended it to the theoretically minded. In recent years it has received substantial support from experiment and observation.

Harnack, A. von A distinguished liberal theologian and church historian, active in the later nineteenth century and early twentieth century.

Hawking black-body radiation Black holes are condensations of matter so dense that their gravitational field would appear strong enough to trap permanently all particles caught inside them. (That is why they are called black, even light cannot escape.) Stephen Hawking showed, however, that quantum theory modifies this and allows even a black hole to shine slightly with what physicists call black-body radiation. (For the learned: this is due to quantum mechanical tunnelling.)

Historical Jesus, the quest of The search to establish the historical figure of Jesus which lies behind the theologically overlaid accounts of the Gospels. The nineteenth century was an era of intense activity in writing lives of Jesus. At the beginning of this century Albert Schweitzer (q.v.) devastatingly showed how many of these writings reflected more of their authors than of their supposed subject. A subsequent reaction set in against the search, with a resulting tendency to declare the historical Jesus inaccessible to us. A more balanced approach, which recognizes the difficulties but does not despair of the task, characterizes the present situation.

Horkheimer, M. A member of the so-called Frankfurt school of philosophers, economists and sociologists, active in the 1920s and influential thereafter.

Hume, D. Eighteenth-century Scottish philosopher in the British empiricist tradition. He wrote with clarity and considerable scepticism both on issues in science (where he criticized the ideas of induction (q.v.) and causality) and in religion (where he criticized any belief in miracles and the classical 'proofs' of the existence of God).

Induction The attempt to establish general laws by the collection of large numbers of particular instances. As a *method* it is indispensable to science (one cannot examine all the electrons in the universe before making a general statement about them) but its logical status has been subject to much critical discussion from David Hume (q.v.) to Karl Popper (q.v.).

Julian of Norwich A late fourteenth-century woman solitary whose remarkable visions and her reflections upon them are recorded in *Revelations of Divine Love*.

Jung, C. G. One of the founders of modern depth psychology in the early years of this century. Originally a colleague of Freud's, he parted from him because of their differing views on the primacy of the sexual drive and the value of religion. One of Jung's most distinctive and controversial contributions is his identification of the collective unconscious, a level of the psyche which goes beyond the individual and which is the repository of archetypes (q.v.).

Kammerlingh Onnes, H. Dutch physicist who in 1911 discovered the phenomenon of superconductivity (q.v.)

Kelvin, Lord (W. H. Thompson) Nineteenth-century physicist particularly associated with the attempt to understand all physical phenomena in terms of mechanical models.

Kingdom of God The rule of God. Christian thought presents it both as present in a hidden form and as also to be revealed in a manifest form. Its proclamation was an important part of Jesus' message.

Lamb shift A very small difference between two adjacent spectral lines of the hydrogen atom which proves to be a critical test of quantum electrodynamics (q.v.). It is named after its first measurer, Willis Lamb.

Landau, L. D. One of the great Russian theoretical physicists of this century.

Laplace, Marquis de French theoretical physicist of the eighteenth and early nineteenth centuries, whose work in celestial mechanics makes him the greatest of Newton's successors.

Loisy, A. Leader of the Roman Catholic modernist movement in France, active at the turn of the century. Eventually he was excommunicated.

Measurement in quantum mechanics Every measurement involves a chain of correlated consequences linking the microscopic system being observed to a signal discernible in the macroscopic everyday world of the laboratory. Despite the enormous successes of quantum theory it is still a matter of unresolved dispute where along that chain, from electron, say, to measuring device to conscious observer, it becomes fixed on a particular occasion what the actual outcome of the measurement is to be. (The theory can only predict the relative probabilities of a variety of possible outcomes.) In other words, it is not understood how the quantum mechanically uncertain world of the microscopic, and the determinate world of the macroscopic, consistently interlock with each other. The transition from one to the other is the level-shift problem referred to in Chapter 3.

Messiah Literally 'the anointed one'; in Greek, *christos*. There was a widespread expectation of such a deliverer, sent by God to liberate and vindicate his people, which took various forms in the popular imagination at the time of Jesus.

Miracle A valuable tradition, present in the New Testament and later Christian theology, places emphasis on miracles as *signs* of God's continual presence and power, and not as mere wonders to provoke astonishment. On that view the value of miracle resides in its significance and not in any inexplicability on natural grounds.

Mysticism A much abused word, often used as if it were equivalent to woolliness and irrationality. Its proper meaning is an immediate experience of God, perceived as union with the ground of being.

Myth Another much abused word. It is not a polite word for a fairy tale but it signifies profound significance conveyed in story form. That leaves open the question of historical truthfulness, which may or may not be present. The story of the fall in the garden of Eden is a powerful myth about the human condition which I do not believe to be historical; the incarnation, on the other hand, is a powerful myth of God's participation in his creation which I believe truly centres on the actual person of the historical Jesus.

Ohm's law see Superconductivity.

Olbers' paradox In the early nineteenth century the German astronomer W. H. M. Olbers pointed out that if (a) the universe were infinite and (b) uniformly populated with stars which (c) had been shining for ever, then the sky at night would be as bright as the surface of a star. Since this was obviously not the case it followed that at least one of the assumptions (a), (b) and (c) was wrong – a brilliant deduction of non-trivial information from a commonplace observation.

Popper, Sir Karl A contemporary philosopher of science who has emphasized that scientific theories cannot be verified by induction but can be falsified by experimental counter-example.

Prigogine, I. A contemporary Belgian theoretical physicist and chemist who is noted for his extension of thermodynamics (q.v.) to cover systems far from equilibrium.

Q A hypothetical document of the first century supposed to be the underlying source of the material common to the Gospels of Matthew and Luke.

Quantum chromodynamics The quantum field theory (q.v.) which is believed to describe the interaction of quarks and gluons (q.v.) and so to provide a fundamental theory of the structure of matter. Its name arises from the fact that quarks and gluons are thought to possess an intrinsic property which has been given the (facetious) name of 'colour'.

Quantum electrodynamics The quantum field theory (q.v.) which describes the interactions of electrons and photons.

Quantum field theory A formalism combining relativity and quantum mechanics and so providing the indispensable theoretical means for discussing the behaviour of elementary particles. Because it is a field theory it has the right form to describe wavelike properties, whilst the addition of quantum properties produces a discrete countability which corresponds to particle behaviour. Thus quantum field theory succeeds in resolving the wave/particle duality (q.v.) paradox.

Quantum mechanics see *Measurement*.

Quarks and gluons Matter is currently believed to be composed of particles called quarks, stuck together by an interaction mediated by particles called (oh dear!) gluons.

Quasars Strange astronomical objects (bright and strongly red-shifted) which most astronomers believe to be very distant, very intense, sources, perhaps deriving their energy from the presence within them of a very massive black hole.

Salvation That act of God which brings wholeness and healing to the flawed condition of humanity.

Schweitzer, A. German theologian, musicologist and doctor, who in 1913 abandoned a brilliant academic career to devote the rest of his life to running a clinic at Lambaréné in French Equatorial Africa.

Seleucids The dynasty founded in the fourth century BC by Seleucus I Nicator, one of Alexander's generals. They ruled over a great part of the Levant.

Sin That flawed character of the human condition which leads to individual wrong acts by men. (That is, sin leads to sins.) Christian theology sees sin as rooted in the creature's alienation from, and repudiation of, his Creator.

Socio-biology The theory that attributes social actions, including altruistic behaviour, to genetic influence.

Son of Man The title apparently used by Jesus of himself.

Soteriology The theological study of the nature and means of salvation (q.v.).

Superconductivity At ordinary temperatures the electric current carried by a metal wire is proportional to the voltage applied (Ohm's law). For some metals, below what is called their critical temperature, this behaviour is suddenly changed and currents can circulate for many hours without any voltage being applied to keep them going. This superconducting state, discovered by Kammerlingh Onnes (q.v.), was eventually explained by Bardeen, Cooper and Schrieffer (q.v.).

Synoptic Gospels The Gospels of Matthew, Mark and Luke, which take a broadly similar view of the life of Jesus. This is largely due to their having much material in common. The *synoptic problem* is the attempt to determine what is the nature of the sources from which this common material may be supposed to be derived.

Theodicy The attempt to justify the ways of God to men; in particular, the search for an understanding of why the creation of a loving and all-powerful God should manifest such suffering and evil.

Thermodynamics The study of energy exchanges in natural systems. Classical thermodynamics is concerned with closed (that is, isolated) systems in thermal equilibrium (that is, at a definite temperature).

$3°K$ background radiation The universe is uniformly full of radio 'noise' corresponding to the emission which would come from a source with the very low temperature of $3°K$. It is believed that this background radiation is the cooled-off residue left behind from events in the early expansion of the universe following the big bang (q.v.).

Torah The Hebrew word for law or teaching; hence the first five books of the Old Testament, traditionally attributed to Moses and containing the divine law for Israel.

Wave/particle duality Microscopic objects, such as electrons or photons, behave sometimes as if they were waves and sometimes as if they were particles. This apparently paradoxical behaviour is now fully understood in terms of quantum field theory (q.v.).

YHWH The tetragrammaton, or divine name in Israelite religion. Hebrew was originally written in consonants only, without vowels. When vowel signs (points) were added to the text the scribes, out of reverence, added to YHWH the vowels appropriate to 'adonai', the word pronounced as a substitute for the unutterable divine name. Misunderstanding of this led to the mistaken belief that the divine name was pronounced Jehovah. It is now believed that the original pronunciation was Yahweh.

Index

New Testament criticism, x, 6, 35, 39–41, 48

New Testament manuscripts, 34–5

Newton, I., 5, 15, 25

observational science, 36

Olbers' paradox, 75, 123

other religions, 104–7, 109

Pannenberg, W., ix

Pascal, B., 13, 15

passion narrative, 39, 70–1, 75

Penzias, A. A., 7

pericope, 39

personal knowledge, 4, 16–18, 21

Peter, 35, 42, 45, 57, 64, 72, 83, 87, 89

phenomenology, 96

Planck, M., 25

Popper, K., 5, 123

possible worlds, 13

prayer, 28, 30

Prigogine, I., 24–5, 123

primitive church, 40, 43, 81

psalmist, 14–15

Q, 38, 123

quantum chromodynamics, x, 52, 123–4

quantum electrodynamics, 33, 124

quantum field theory, 26, 33, 67, 124

quantum mechanics, 10, 21–4, 120, 122

quarks and gluons, x, 1, 4, 10, 93, 124

quasar, 36, 57, 124

regimes, 10, 55, 79

relativity, cultural, 18, 49, 105, 108

Rembrandt, 17

Renan, E., 88

resurrection appearances, 82–4, 89

resurrection of all men, 78, 86, 90–4

resurrection of Jesus, 55, 78–80, 85–90, 110

salvation, 75, 90, 106, 124

scandal of particularity, 107

Schweitzer, A., 52–3, 60, 120, 124

science and religion compared, ix–x, 3–4, 11, 36, 55, 67, 80

science, completeness of, 15

sin, 77, 124–5

Sitz im Leben, 39–40

socio-biology, 19, 125

Socrates, 70

solidarity, human, 50, 64, 76

Son of Man, 57–9, 65, 125

soteriology, 6, 125

spirits, 50

suffering, 20, 73, 91, 106, 111

superconductivity, 55, 125

synoptic Gospels, 37, 46, 56, 71, 101, 125

synoptic problem, 37–8, 125

Teresa of Calcutta, 29

theodicy, 21, 73, 91–2, 111, 125

theory and experiment, 5, 80, 96, 98–9

third day, 81, 87

3°K radiation, 7, 125

torah, 61, 125–6